Barbara Kam (l) and Nora Bryan (r)
JUDE DILLON

About the Authors

Barbara Kam and Nora Bryan are avid prairie gardeners who practice what they preach when it comes to creating and enjoying winterscapes. Familiar with the long, cold winters that define who we are and what we do on the prairies, they have created beautiful garden vignettes that can be admired from the warmth of indoors all winter long. Both Barbara and Nora are also active, long-time supporters of The Calgary Horticultural Society and regular contributors to *Calgary Gardening*, an informative members' publication.

Barbara, who holds a Prairie Horticulture Certificate, is the owner of Edenscapes, a garden services company devoted to soft landscape instal-lations and the on-going stewardship of established gardens. An award-winning gardener herself, Barbara enjoys bringing smiles through beauty to her clients.

Nora is the co-author of *The Prairie Gardener's Book of Bugs: A Guide to Living with Common Garden Insects.* This popular backyard viewing guide was written to help prairie gardeners identify and understand garden bugs. Also a columnist for the *Calgary Herald*, Nora draws on her background in natural sciences and experience working at a large garden centre to share her knowledge with fellow gardeners.

The plants described in this book perform well in gardens in the Canadian prairies and the northern Great Plains of the United States.

The Prairie
WINTERSCAPE
CREATIVE GARDENING
FOR THE FORGOTTEN SEASON

BARBARA KAM AND NORA BRYAN

FIFTH
HOUSE

Cover and interior design by Articulate Eye
Front cover photo by Michael Interisano
Scans by St. Solo Computer Graphics
Edited/copyedited by Geri Rowlatt
Proofread by Ann Sullivan

The publisher gratefully acknowledges the support of The Canada Council for the Arts and the Department of Canadian Heritage.

THE CANADA COUNCIL | LE CONSEIL DES ARTS
FOR THE ARTS | DU CANADA
SINCE 1957 | DEPUIS 1957

We acknowledge the financial support of the Government of Canada through the Book Publishing Industry Development Program (BPIDP) for our publishing activities.

Printed in Canada by Friesens

03 04 05 06 07 / 5 4 3 2 1

National Library of Canada Cataloguing in Publication Data

Kam, Barbara, 1962–
The Prairie Winterscape: Creative Gardening for the Forgotten Season / by Barbara Kam and Nora Bryan.

Includes bibliographical references and index.
ISBN 1-894856-08-2

1. Winter gardening—Prairie Provinces. 2. Landscape gardening—Prairie Provinces. I. Bryan, Nora, 1959– II. Title.
SB439.5.K35 2003 635.9'53 C2003-910440-0

Fifth House Ltd.
A Fitzhenry & Whiteside Company
1511, 1800 - 4 St. SW
Calgary, Alberta T2S 2S5
1-800-387-9776
www.fitzhenry.ca

First published in the United States in 2004 by
Fitzhenry & Whiteside
121 Harvard Avenue, Suite 2
Allston, MA 02134

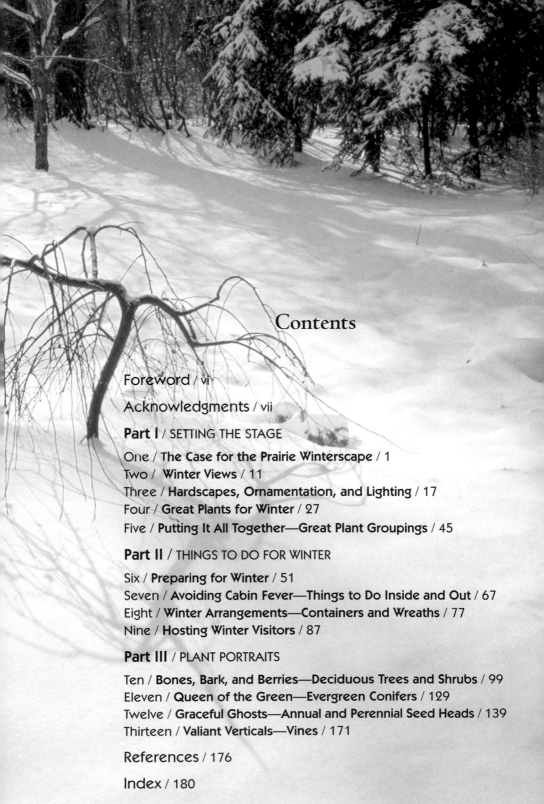

Contents

Foreword

Winter—from November's overture, through its full-blown January and February presence, to a slow April exit—occupies over half of the prairie gardener's year. This is reason enough for a book as thorough and lively as *The Prairie Winterscape*. Barbara Kam and Nora Bryan make a convincing case for including the often forgotten season in garden planning and planting—and then show you how to do it.

As the authors note, the beauty of the winter garden resides in the subtleties of bark and berries, the shades and shapes of evergreens, and the "graceful ghosts" of summer seed heads and grass plumes. All are detailed in comprehensive lists of shrubs, trees, vines, and perennials that contribute to the winter landscape. The discussion of design ensures that chosen plants will be seen in the best light possible—even if it is the low light of short winter days.

A garden, though, is more than just plants, and never more so than in winter, when ornamentation and outdoor arrangements of boughs and branches come into their own. There is magic, too, and a kind of poignancy to outdoor lights in winter—the authors tell you all you need to know about lighting winter paths safely and effectively. And what would the cold, dark season be without the cheerful swoop and chatter of birds? Dip into the chapter on feeders and food to draw in feathered friends.

With enthusiasm, knowledge, and obvious passion for the prairies, Kam and Bryan have put together a book that is sure to inspire readers to reconsider, or perhaps even to consider for the first time, their view of the garden in winter.

Plan for winter beauty, and the scene framed by windows overlooking the garden is bound to be better year round.

Patrick Lima
Larkwhistle, Ontario

Acknowledgments

When telling people about the subject of our book, we consistently met with one of two responses: an enthused "It's about time!" or a confused, "But nothing grows here …" We are delighted to have an opportunity to explain our point of view to the skeptics and looking back, this opportunity could not exist without the efforts and assistance of many people. We wish to "tip our toques" in gratitude to the following people:

Liesbeth Leatherbarrow, Lesley Reynolds, and Charlene Dobmeier for believing that the phrase "the winter prairie garden" is a concept worth sharing with others and *not* an oxymoron.

The many kind and skeptical gardeners who spoke with us and/or let us tromp through their gardens in the depths of winter: Ramza Barbary, Margaret Brown, Ida DeJong, Judith Doyle, Mary-Leigh Doyle, Jackie Flanagan, Trish Hines, Nina Kilpatrick, Iris Maillot, Birgitta and Jim Mick, Morsky Family, Shirley Scott, Rod Shaver, Llyn Strelau, Maureen Wagner, Joyce Watson, Andy Wicherts, and others who wish to remain anonymous. There are also gardeners with lovely front yards where we shamelessly took pictures in admiration. To all the gardeners, thank-you for making our frosty world a little more beautiful.

Our expert readers Wayne Bishop, Paul Harris, Olivia Johns, Birgitta Mick, and Terry Warke—we are grateful for your insights, suggestions, and the experience you give to our book; Michael Interisano for our cover shot that captures the concept of winterscaping in a halo of hoarfrost; Victoria Goddard for gathering weather data; the keen gardeners on the Calgary Horticultural Society chatline and Garden Web's Far North Garden Forum for answering questions.

"Mother Nature" for having such varied faces, even within a single season, each offering its own unique beauty. We wonder why most of the good days for photography had to be so darn cold. Bitter cold holds few comforts for intrepid photographers and may be the prime reason that so few books on winter gardens exist where there actually *is* a winter.

Our family and friends for their support throughout and for their patience as we changed plans on short notice on frosty days to get "just a few more shots."

Finally, this book would not exist with out the commitment and guidance from the team provided by Fifth House Publishing: Charlene, Liesbeth and Lesley (again), Simone Lee, Geri Rowlatt, Joan Tetrault, Ann Sullivan, and Brian Smith and Mike McCoy at Articulate Eye.

An attractive garden photographed in late summer (above) and again in mid-winter (below). NORA BRYAN

One

The Case for the Prairie Winterscape

AFTER THE FIRST KILLING FROST, diligent prairie gardeners "put the garden to bed." We chop back perennials, bury borderline-hardy plants under thick, warm blankets of leaves or compost, and put pots, ornaments, and tools back in the shed. For most of us, our once living, colorful outdoor space becomes a boring horizontal plane relieved only by piles of mulch. It is as if the landscape ceases to exist as we move our lives indoors. But it need not be so. We can let our gardens remain dull and uninspiring in winter or we can transform them into magical places that we can enjoy from the comfort of our warm houses. Shape, texture, color, movement, sound, and dramatic shadow are in the winter landscape, waiting to be discovered. Although savvy prairie gardeners lengthen the growing season by choosing plants that tolerate light frosts, it is possible to find plants that look good in the depths of winter. You can also make your garden an attractive place for birds that overwinter on the prairies.

This book is about creating an all-season northern prairie garden. In addition to detailed plant profiles, it provides design ideas, projects, and appropriate gardening techniques to help you create your own winterscape. Some of the ideas may seem heretical, flying in the face of conventional wisdom about what constitute appropriate gardening techniques. Other ideas may challenge your definition of beauty. But, as you read through this book, we encourage you to consider the possibility and the art of the winterscape.

The plants described in this book are found in the Canadian prairies, from the eastern edge of the Rocky Mountains, through the southern half of Alberta, Saskatchewan, and Manitoba, and into the northern Great Plains of the United States.

The Prairie Winter

Across the prairie region, the average continuous frost-free period is shorter than the period that can get frost (see Table 1). Daytime temperatures may be above freezing in mid-autumn and early spring, but evenings bring frost. January and February are typically not only the coldest months on the prairies (see Table 2), but also when the ground "lightens up" with the most persistent snowfall (see Table 3). Snowfall in March and April may be greater, but it melts more readily. It is as though prairie gardeners have two winter seasons: the first predominantly brown, the second, white.

Winters can be very different from one year to the next. Some are warmer than average, while others are bitterly cold for long stretches of time. After nestling under a blanket of snow most of one winter, gardens can be left dry and brown most of another. In dry years, we experience a longer "no grow but no snow" period, with beige lawns, exposed soil, and an increased probability of a brown Christmas.

Although winter varies its charms and trials each year, the winterscape also relates the story of the past growing year. Abundant leaves remaining on trees and shrubs tell of early killing frosts. Deep red and russet leaves that linger speak of warmer, sunnier autumns. Evergreens turning beige cry out, condemning dry falls.

Inspiration

Instead of enduring the many months to the next frost-free period, why not acknowledge the short winter days and cold temperatures of the "dark side" of our climate? There are many plants that continue to enchant with their form, bark, seeds, or berries. It's a long, long season, but it doesn't have to be bleak.

Perhaps part of the reason why the prairie garden in winter has been ignored is the dearth of inspiring, relevant literature on the subject. Books on winter gardening aren't written for regions where daily routines include clearing snow and chiseling ice from windshields. They come from England or warmer parts of Canada or the United States where there may be only a few days with frost. These books show winter containers of pansies and parsley and suggest which plants to select for scent in January. Oh, please! Glossy pictures and lists of non-hardy "recommended" plants taunt prairie gardeners, leading to resignation. It is no wonder the northern winter garden has been sadly ignored.

We say, forget those books. Hellebores and boxwood hedges aside, concepts of harmony and balance, and even plant choices, are transferable to the prairie garden year-round. Let's accept that we have our own regional style of winter elegance and that there is beauty in the promise of rebirth and in the knowledge that winter is part of nature's cycle. Prairie gardeners can foster a prairie style of beauty in the cold season—it's just a matter of desire and inspiration.

A Prairie Winterscape

Winter's colors may not be riotous, but they do have a subtle beauty. Sepia tints and tones of gray dominate the landscape. Just as the drama of black-and-white photographs can be appreciated as a distinct art form from color pictures, the elegant palette of winter can be admired as distinct from summer's Technicolor™. A dab of red rose hips, the glowing copper bark of a mountain ash, the deep green skirts of a conifer laced with snow positioned against sophisticated neutrals—this is the stuff of winter beauty.

A good winter garden has much more than just color, though. Shape, texture, movement, and sound are all part of it. From arbors to vines, shapes are stronger and more graphic in winter. The lower angle of the sun casts dramatic shadows. Mounds of plant debris spared from winter cleanup allude to what once was and what can be again. Textures we rarely notice in summer come to the fore. The deeply ribbed bark of a mature laurel leaf willow or a poplar is cast in sharp relief under the oblique winter sun. The curling and exfoliating bark of the Amur cherry against a brilliant winter day is an arresting sight. Movement is present in the swaying plumes and rustling leaves of ornamental grasses. Birds rarely noticed amongst the summer leaf canopy of our trees delight us with their movements and calls. The pleasant tinkling of water into the pond is still possible, given some preparation, and prairie winds still invite chimes to ring. Sound lives in the winter garden too.

Easy Joy

One of the greatest joys of a winter garden on the prairies is that once your initial planning and set-up are complete, it need only be enjoyed from the comfort of your home. It is truly a different way to garden. After the intense growing season, when plants seem to grow in front of your eyes, winter gardening is about setting scenes. Winterscaping works, even for the somewhat lazy or burnt-out summer gardener, as there is little actual yard work to be done beyond shoveling snow. Indeed, the basics of winterscaping are few in number.

Avoid "Make Work"

Some fall cleanup is merely "make work." For instance, many gardeners chop perennials down in fall, only trim them back still lower in spring. However, if left through the winter, many perennial tops either will have disintegrated or will come off with an easy tug by spring. These same gardeners likely also rake garden beds clean of leaves and then apply winter mulch, another ritual of fall cleanup. Yet, come spring, winter winds will have blown debris back into the beds and they will need to be raked once again. Winterscaping allows you to forego these types of chores, without guilt, and lets you focus on only what truly needs to be done.

Don't Sweat the Small Stuff

Since winter gardens are primarily about views, it's the big stuff that counts. Anything installed specifically for outdoor appreciation, like winter container arrangements, must be bold to be noticed, not fussy. Fussing over subtle textures of groundcovers can be forgotten. There is no lawn to mow. Generally, any plant less than a foot tall can be selected purely on its summer merits. For winter, you're interested in tall, sturdy plants that won't be defeated by snow.

What You See Is What You Work

Look at the front entry of your house, the front of the garage, the trash haul trek, and the views from the windows you look out of the most. These are your winter sight lines and the basis of your winter garden. Parts of the garden that are visible during the summer from decks or patios are often invisible during the winter. Preparing a winter garden is a much smaller job in terms of area compared with a summer garden.

No Fuss, No Bother

Plants are dormant. It's cold, particularly in January and February. There is no need to fuss with fertilizing or deadheading. There are no bugs, no rust, no aphids eating your leaves, and no chemicals with which to contend.

TABLE I: FROST-FREE PERIOD

Location	Average continuous frost-free period (days)	Days outside continuous frost-free period	% of year outside continuous frost-free period
Calgary, AB	112	253	69.3%
Edmonton, AB	140	225	61.6%
Lethbridge, AB	124	241	66.0%
Red Deer, AB	109	256	70.1%
Estevan, SK	124	241	66.0%
Regina, SK	109	256	70.1%
Saskatoon, SK	117	248	67.9%
Swift Current, SK	118	247	67.7%
Brandon, MB	108	257	70.4%
Morden, MB	129	236	64.7%
Winnipeg, MB	121	244	66.8%
Crookston, MN	124	241	66.0%
Fergus Falls, MN	141	224	61.4%
Marshall, MN	153	212	58.1%
Billings, MT	133	232	63.6%
Great Falls, MT*	112	253	69.3%
Helena, MT	122	243	66.6%
Lewistown, MT	116	249	68.2%
Miles City, MT	138	227	62.2%
Chadron, NE	132	233	63.8%
Bismarck, ND*	127	238	65.2%
Dickinson, ND	132	233	63.8%
Fargo, ND*	137	228	62.5%
Grand Forks, ND	123	242	66.3%
Jamestown, ND	127	238	65.2%
Minot, ND	127	238	65.2%
Pierre, SD*	138	227	62.2%
Rapid City, SD	147	218	59.7%
Sioux Falls, SD	143	222	60.8%
Casper, WY	121	244	66.8%
Sheridan, WY	123	242	66.3%

SOURCES

Environment Canada. *Canadian Climate Normals*, Volume 6, Frost (1951–1980).

American data from The National Climatic Data Center, *Climatography of the U.S.* No. 20, Supplement No. 1, Freeze/Frost Data, January 1988, pp. 47, 73–76, 86–96, 116–19, 141–45, 179–82 (Online)

* Indicates sites with data interpolated from the nearest weather stations participating in the American study.

TABLE 2: AVERAGE MINIMUM TEMPERATURE °C (°F)

Location	Oct °C (°F)	Nov °C (°F)	Dec °C (°F)	Jan °C (°F)	Feb °C (°F)	Mar °C (°F)	Apr °C (°F)
Calgary, AB	-1.4 (29.5)	-8.9 (16.0)	-13.4 (7.9)	-15.1 (4.8)	-12.0 (10.4)	-7.8 (18.0)	-2.1 (28.2)
Edmonton, AB	0.3 (32.5)	-8.2 (17.2)	-13.9 (7.0)	-16.0 (3.2)	-13.1 (8.4)	-7.3 (18.9)	-0.3 (31.5)
Lethbridge, AB	0.0 (32.0)	-7.2 (19.0)	-12.0 (10.4)	-13.8 (7.2)	-10.7 (12.7)	-6.5 (20.3)	-0.9 (30.4)
Red Deer, AB	-1.3 (29.7)	-9.4 (15.1)	-15.0 (5.0)	-17.4 (0.7)	-14.8 (5.4)	-8.8 (16.2)	-1.8 (28.8)
Estevan, SK	-1.0 (30.2)	-9.4 (15.1)	-16.9 (1.6)	-20.1 (-4.2)	-15.5 (4.1)	-9.0 (15.8)	-1.6 (29.1)
Regina, SK	-2.0 (28.4)	-10.7 (12.7)	-18.5 (-1.3)	-21.6 (-6.9)	-17.1 (1.2)	-10.3 (13.5)	-2.0 (28.4)
Saskatoon, SK	-1.9 (28.6)	-10.9 (12.4)	-19.3 (-2.7)	-22.3 (-8.1)	-18.2 (-0.8)	-10.9 (12.4)	-1.9 (28.6)
Swift Current, SK	-1.3 (29.7)	-9.3 (15.3)	-15.6 (3.9)	-17.2 (1.0)	-14.6 (5.7)	-8.3 (17.1)	-1.6 (29.1)
Brandon, MB	-2.1 (28.2)	-11.1 (12.0)	-20.0 (-4.0)	-23.5 (-10.3)	-19.3 (-2.7)	-11.8 (10.8)	-2.9 (26.8)
Morden, MB	1.3 (34.3)	-16.6 (2.1)	-17.2 (1.0)	-20.1 (-4.2)	-16.2 (2.8)	-9.2 (15.4)	-1.0 (30.2)
Winnipeg, MB	-0.3 (31.5)	-9.6 (14.7)	-19.1 (-2.4)	-22.8 (-9.0)	-18.7 (-1.7)	-11.0 (12.2)	-2.4 (27.7)
Crookston, MN	1.2 (34.1)	-7.7 (18.1)	-16.4 (2.5)	-21.0 (-5.8)	-18.5 (-1.3)	-10.2 (13.6)	-0.8 (30.6)
Fergus Falls, MN	2.2 (35.9)	-6.3 (20.7)	-14.8 (5.3)	-19.4 (-3.0)	-15.7 (3.7)	-8.4 (16.9)	0.0 (32.0)
Marshall, MN	3.3 (37.9)	-4.8 (23.3)	-12.4 (9.7)	-16.3 (2.7)	-12.6 (9.3)	-6.3 (20.6)	1.4 (34.6)
Billings, MT	2.9 (37.3)	-3.4 (25.9)	-7.8 (18.0)	-10.3 (13.5)	-6.9 (19.5)	-4.0 (24.8)	1.1 (33.9)
Great Falls, MT	2.3 (36.1)	-3.5 (25.7)	-7.3 (18.8)	-10.2 (13.7)	-9.7 (14.5)	-5.6 (22.0)	0.7 (33.2)
Helena, MT	0.7 (33.3)	-5.3 (22.4)	-9.6 (14.7)	-11.6 (11.1)	-9.3 (15.3)	-5.4 (22.3)	-0.1 (31.8)

Lewistown, MT	-0.2 (31.7)	-5.6 (22.0)	-9.4 (15.0)	-15.3 (4.4)	-10.0 (14.0)	-9.7 (14.6)	-3.1 (26.5)
Miles City, MT	1.7 (35.1)	-5.3 (22.4)	-11.1 (12.1)	-14.6 (5.7)	-12.3 (9.8)	-6.1 (21.1)	1.2 (34.1)
Chadron, NE	1.3 (34.3)	-5.6 (22.0)	-10.4 (13.3)	-18.4 (-1.2)	-14.3 (6.3)	-8.4 (16.9)	-0.6 (31.0)
Bismarck, ND	0.3 (32.5)	-7.8 (18.0)	-15.1 (4.8)	-19.1 (-2.4)	-14.7 (5.5)	-8.3 (17.1)	-0.8 (30.5)
Dickinson, ND	0.6 (33.1)	-7.1 (19.2)	-13.1 (8.4)	-16.3 (2.7)	-12.5 (9.5)	-7.9 (17.7)	-1.2 (29.8)
Fargo, ND	1.7 (35.0)	-7.0 (19.4)	-15.4 (4.2)	-19.6 (-3.2)	-16.0 (3.2)	-8.4 (16.9)	0.0 (32.0)
Grand Forks, ND	0.8 (33.4)	-7.8 (17.9)	-16.6 (2.1)	-21.0 (-5.8)	-17.1 (1.2)	-9.6 (14.8)	-0.7 (30.7)
Jamestown, ND	0.8 (33.5)	-7.6 (18.3)	-15.2 (4.6)	-19.2 (-2.5)	-15.2 (4.6)	-8.6 (16.6)	-0.8 (30.6)
Minot, ND	1.3 (34.4)	-7.2 (19.1)	-14.2 (6.4)	-18.4 (-1.2)	-14.3 (6.3)	-8.4 (16.9)	-0.6 (31.0)
Pierre, SD	1.7 (35.0)	-6.1 (21.0)	-12.0 (10.4)	-13.9 (7.0)	-8.4 (16.8)	-4.8 (23.4)	0.6 (33.1)
Rapid City, SD	2.8 (37.0)	-4.2 (24.5)	-8.7 (16.3)	-11.0 (12.2)	-8.4 (16.9)	-5.1 (22.8)	0.5 (32.9)
Sioux Falls, SD	2.6 (36.7)	-5.4 (22.3)	-12.3 (9.8)	-15.8 (3.6)	-11.9 (10.5)	-5.8 (21.6)	1.3 (34.4)
Casper, WY	0.4 (32.7)	-5.5 (22.1)	-9.4 (15.0)	-10.8 (12.5)	-8.6 (16.6)	-5.8 (21.6)	-1.4 (29.4)
Sheridan, WY	0.0 (32.0)	-6.7 (20.0)	-11.2 (11.8)	-12.9 (8.7)	-9.7 (14.5)	-6.1 (21.1)	-0.8 (30.5)

SOURCES

Environment Canada. Canadian Climate Normals 1971–2000 (Created 17 December 2002; modified 2 January 2003). Retrieved 7 January 2003 from http://www.msc-smc.ec.gc.ca/climate/climate_normals/index_e.cfm

American data from University of Nebraska, High Plains Regional Climatic Center (Online). Available at www.hprcc.unl.edu

TABLE 3: SNOW DEPTH*

Location	Oct cm (in.)	Nov cm (in.)	Dec cm (in.)	Jan cm (in.)	Feb cm (in.)	Mar cm (in.)	Apr cm (in.)
Calgary, AB	1.0 (0.4)	4.0 (1.6)	5.0 (2.0)	5.0 (2.0)	3.0 (1.2)	2.0 (0.8)	0.0 (0.0)
Edmonton, AB	1.0 (0.4)	6.0 (2.4)	15.0 (5.9)	21.0 (8.3)	19.0 (7.5)	5.0 (2.0)	0.0 (0.0)
Lethbridge, AB	1.0 (0.4)	2.0 (0.8)	5.0 (2.0)	6.0 (2.4)	3.0 (1.2)	3.0 (1.2)	0.0 (0.0)
Red Deer, AB	1.0 (0.4)	7.0 (2.8)	15.0 (5.9)	20.0 (7.9)	15.0 (5.9)	6.0 (2.4)	0.0 (0.0)
Estevan, SK	1.0 (0.4)	5.0 (2.0)	11.0 (4.3)	14.0 (5.5)	13.0 (5.1)	2.0 (0.8)	0.0 (0.0)
Regina, SK	1.0 (0.4)	7.0 (2.8)	15.0 (5.9)	19.0 (7.5)	16.0 (6.3)	5.0 (2.0)	0.0 (0.0)
Saskatoon, SK	2.0 (0.8)	5.0 (2.0)	12.0 (4.7)	17.0 (6.7)	14.0 (5.5)	3.0 (1.2)	0.0 (0.0)
Swift Current, SK	1.0 (0.4)	4.0 (1.6)	8.0 (3.1)	9.0 (3.5)	9.0 (3.5)	3.0 (1.2)	1.0 (0.4)
Brandon, MB	2.0 (0.8)	7.0 (2.8)	15.0 (5.9)	22.0 (8.7)	19.0 (7.5)	6.0 (2.4)	0.0 (0.0)
Morden, MB	2.0 (0.8)	8.0 (3.1)	12.0 (4.7)	16.0 (6.3)	16.0 (6.3)	10.0 (3.9)	1.0 (0.4)
Winnipeg, MB	2.0 (0.8)	8.0 (3.1)	14.0 (5.5)	20.0 (7.9)	19.0 (7.5)	7.0 (2.8)	0.0 (0.0)
Crookston, MN	0.0 (0.0)	2.5 (1.0)	10.2 (4.0)	20.3 (8.0)	17.8 (7.0)	10.2 (4.0)	0.0 (0.0)
Fergus Falls, MN	0.0 (0.0)	2.5 (1.0)	10.2 (4.0)	22.9 (9.0)	22.9 (9.0)	12.7 (5.0)	0.0 (0.0)
Marshall, MN	0.0 (0.0)	2.5 (1.0)	7.6 (3.0)	12.7 (5.0)	15.2 (6.0)	10.2 (4.0)	0.0 (0.0)
Billings, MT	0.0 (0.0)	2.5 (1.0)	5.1 (2.0)	7.6 (3.0)	5.1 (2.0)	2.5 (1.0)	0.0 (0.0)
Great Falls, MT	0.0 (0.0)	2.5 (1.0)	5.1 (2.0)	5.1 (2.0)	7.6 (3.0)	2.5 (1.0)	0.0 (0.0)
Helena, MT	2.5 (1.0)	12.7 (5.0)	25.4 (10.0)	33.0 (13.0)	30.5 (12.0)	12.7 (5.0)	2.5 (1.0)
Lewistown, MT	0.0 (0.0)	2.5 (1.0)	5.1 (2.0)	12.7 (5.0)	10.2 (4.0)	10.2 (4.0)	2.5 (1.0)
Miles City, MT	0.0 (0.0)	2.5 (1.0)	5.1 (2.0)	7.6 (3.0)	7.6 (3.0)	2.5 (1.0)	0.0 (0.0)
Chadron, NE	0.0 (0.0)	2.5 (1.0)	2.5 (1.0)	5.1 (2.0)	5.1 (2.0)	2.5 (1.0)	0.0 (0.0)
Bismarck, ND	0.0 (0.0)	2.5 (1.0)	7.6 (3.0)	10.2 (4.0)	10.2 (4.0)	5.1 (2.0)	0.0 (0.0)

Dickinson, ND	0.0 (0.0)	2.5 (1.0)	5.1 (2.0)	7.6 (3.0)	7.6 (3.0)	5.1 (2.0)	2.5 (1.0)
Grand Forks, ND	0.0 (0.0)	2.5 (1.0)	10.2 (4.0)	17.8 (7.0)	17.8 (7.0)	10.2 (4.0)	0.0 (0.0)
Fargo, ND	0.0 (0.0)	2.5 (1.0)	7.6 (3.0)	15.2 (6.0)	15.2 (6.0)	10.2 (4.0)	0.0 (0.0)
Jamestown, ND	0.0 (0.0)	2.5 (1.0)	7.6 (3.0)	15.2 (6.0)	12.7 (5.0)	7.6 (3.0)	2.5 (1.0)
Minot, ND	0.0 (0.0)	2.5 (1.0)	7.6 (3.0)	15.2 (6.0)	12.7 (5.0)	7.6 (3.0)	2.5 (1.0)
Pierre, SD	0.0 (0.0)	2.5 (1.0)	5.1 (2.0)	5.1 (2.0)	7.6 (3.0)	5.1 (2.0)	0.0 (0.0)
Rapid City, SD	0.0 (0.0)	0.0 (1.0)	5.1 (2.0)	5.1 (2.0)	7.6 (3.0)	5.1 (2.0)	0.0 (0.0)
Sioux Falls, SD	0.0 (0.0)	2.5 (1.0)	5.1 (2.0)	10.2 (4.0)	10.2 (4.0)	7.6 (3.0)	0.0 (0.0)
Casper, WY	0.0 (0.0)	2.5 (1.0)	2.5 (1.0)	2.5 (1.0)	2.5 (1.0)	2.5 (1.0)	0.0 (0.0)
Sheridan, WY	0.0 (0.0)	2.5 (1.0)	5.1 (2.0)	7.6 (3.0)	7.6 (3.0)	2.5 (1.0)	0.0 (0.0)

Sources: Environment Canada. Canadian Climate Normals 1971–2000 (Created 17 December 2002; modified 2 January 2003). Retrieved 7 January 2003 from http://www.msc-smc.ec.gc.ca/climate/climate_normals/index_e.cfm

American data from University of Nebraska, High Plains Regional Climatic Center (online). Available at www.hprcc.unl.edu Data period varies depending on site.

Achieve a vibrant winter view using plants with a variety of heights, textures, and colors.
NORA BRYAN

*Note: American locations show average snow depth, Canadian locations show month-end snow cover. American data sources reported in whole inches only; Canadian data sources reported in the smaller increment of centimeter (1 in. = 2.54 cm).

Two

Winter Views

How do you make a garden look good in winter? You start with good design and build from there. Although most of us know what we like when we see it, we can't always identify the "special something" that separates an okay garden from an appealing one. Understanding a few basic design concepts will increase the likelihood of achieving that special something, whether you want to redesign your whole garden or just create some artful winter scenes to admire from your window.

Great gardens have two things in common: harmony and balance. A sense of harmony and balance is achieved in the garden by using the design principles of repetition, contrast, and focal points. The building blocks of your vision include mass, texture, shape, color, and movement and sound. The principles of good design remain the same, regardless of season or personal taste. And, despite our long non-growing season, winter design does not take precedence over the other seasons; instead, it is integrated into the overall design.

Harmony and Balance

Harmony creates a sense of wholeness and belonging, much like a unifying theme. Look at your garden. Do the various parts seem to belong with each other? Does the garden belong to the house? You can unite your home and garden by repeating house materials in the hard landscape or by bringing the shapes or colors of your house into the garden. Link various parts of the garden by incorporating similar hard materials or by repeating shapes or plants throughout it.

Balance describes a sense of equilibrium and appropriate proportion amongst garden elements. To achieve balance, you must consider proportion and visual weight. Have you ever walked into a garden in which all

The classic combination of mugo pine and rose hips works equally well in the garden bed or in a winter container arrangement.
NORA BRYAN

the "action" was concentrated on only one half of the garden? Did you feel like you might tip over? Balance hinges on a pivot point or fulcrum, much like children on a teeter-totter. In the landscape, the fulcrum can be a door, a patio, or a focal point.

Visual weight is the sense of heaviness that we attach to garden elements. The size, color, texture, and apparent mass of an object all impact an object's visual weight and determine to what extent an object appears to dominate or influence the sense of balance in a design. Generally, larger size, darker color, coarser texture, and substantial mass convey heaviness. The opposite suggests something lighter.

Repetition

Repetition contributes to harmony in the garden. Repeating color, texture, mass, form, plant groupings, or hard materials throughout the space leads the eye to create interconnection. In winter, although pathways, arbors, fences, and trees and shrubs remain visible, much of the softscape (plants) is flattened or removed. This makes the repetition of hard materials and woody ornamentals even more important for achieving a sense of harmony.

The goal of repetition is linkage and rhythm. Position a few Siberian coral dogwoods throughout your garden to lead the eye along, creating a sense of harmony. Or repeat the rectangular shape of the panes of a French door in the pattern of the sidewalk, container shape, or grid of a trellis to link the house and garden together.

Contrast

Contrast addresses the risk of monotonous repetition by creating interest and excitement through visual tension. Juxtaposing different colors, textures, heights, and shapes highlights each object's uniqueness. Ironically, too much contrast creates visual noise rather than interest. Of course, the risk of garden chaos is higher in summer because of the greater variety of plant materials and colors.

Curiously, winter has a repeated color contrast—light and dark—that binds the garden cohesively. Creating unity in the winter garden is almost done for you! However, black and white is not enough if the contrast remains solely on the horizontal plane. In winter, you must strive for contrast in texture and with other colors since the material choices, though varied, are subtle and limited compared to summer. One way to create effective contrast in color and texture is to couple evergreens with the jewels of berried treasures.

Focal Points

Focal points are highlights, or accents, in the garden that draw your eye. A focal point can be a hard structure like an arbor or sculpture, a winter container, or a compelling arrangement of plants. Each view has only one focal point; otherwise, the eye does not know where to rest. Because what is in view during summer may be out of sight in winter, you may need to relocate some items to create focal points visible from inside. During the dark of winter, using night lighting to enhance focal points can be particularly striking.

Building Blocks of Design

Mass

Density and porosity, the solidness or openness of an object, are opposing elements on the mass continuum. Solid objects appear weightier than open or porous ones, but it is a relative concept. A mugo pine appears open next to a spruce tree, yet dense compared with the open habit of dogwood or perennial Joe Pye weed.

Texture

Texture is about roughness or smoothness. It includes both the actual feel and the visual effect of surfaces. Generally, coarse-textured objects are large, dark, dull, hairy, or rough. Visually, they appear bold, strong, and heavy.

This yellow pine and blue spruce repeat each other's conical shape, but contrast in color and density.
NORA BRYAN

Fine-textured objects are glossy, small, lighter in color, and smooth; they have a delicate effect. Textures can be repeated for unity or contrasted for variation. You can make a space more intimate by placing coarse and dense objects in the distance and finer-textured plants close to viewing or seating areas. The reverse is also true.

Shape
Plants and hard landscaping have basic shapes. Think in terms of squares, circles, and triangles (fan or cone shaped). A change in the dimensions of these basic shapes results in rectangles, ovals, and broad or narrow triangles. Tall and narrow shapes draw the eye up, while wider objects draw the eye out. Shapes can be layered by size, massed, repeated, or contrasted to achieve various effects.

Color
Even exuberant summer gardens include white, silver, and lots of green to rest the eye between jolts of pink and orange. In winter, snow cover gives the eye plenty of resting space. Bark and branches show grays and browns, while the ghostly vestiges of perennials and annuals weather to parchment, biscuit, taupe, or umber, their brightness long since frozen from their being. The landscape is a quiet contrast of dark and light relieved primarily by sepia tints. A gardener interested in beautifying the winterscape can brighten the palette. In most summer gardens, green is a neutral background color. In winter, green's various tints and tones come to the forefront. Green enhances the reds, yellows, and oranges of berries, bark, and outdoor ornamentation, making each color seem brighter.

Movement and Sound
In a landscape where everything appears frozen in place, movement and sound are lively contradictions that offer hope that we can endure the long cold season. Movement comes from the swaying of defiant perennials or branches and the birds that flit from branch to branch, especially if we provide extra food (see Chapter Nine). Our ears are treated to the rustling of wind, wind chimes, birdcalls, or trickling water.

The Rule of Thirds
Too often, the principles of balance and proportion, so carefully considered for summer, are forgotten about or ignored in the winter garden.

When it comes to northern gardening, a good principle for an attractive year-round garden is the "rule of thirds," that is, approximately one-third of your plantings should be evergreens; another third, deciduous shrubs and trees; and the final third, annuals and perennials. Although this rule is more of a guideline, it addresses intuitively several of the design principles that are noted above. With roughly two-thirds of your plantings devoted to shrubs and trees, you automatically have some repetition and contrast in mass, shape, texture, and color.

The ephemeral nature of perennials and annuals combined with the seasonality and variability of deciduous woody ornamentals emphasizes the need to include structures, focal points, and suitable trees and shrubs in the northern garden. Gardens composed largely of perennials and annuals can look barren in early spring, late autumn, and winter. Once plants are felled by frost or chopped down, a house that was solidly anchored by a lush summer landscape can appear barely pinned in place if only a few scraggly foundation shrubs are visible during winter. Indeed, an expanse of wall fronted by a small number of meager plants appears to be a waste of plants. However, gardens that lean heavily toward evergreens may feel somber and imposing during the summer, while those heavily weighted with perennials and deciduous woody ornamentals will seem to be missing something in their understory during summer and lack visual punch during winter. Provide your garden with year-round flair by using a variety of conifers and deciduous trees and shrubs and an assortment of herbaceous plants in amongst your garden's permanent structures.

The rule of thirds also applies to height: tall, medium, and short. Much like three rows of children lined up by height for a school photo, place the tall materials at the back and the short plants at the front so you can see all their faces. This guideline helps a gardener include contrast and variation in height, which contributes to a sense of depth and enclosure and allows each treasure to be seen.

The concepts of harmony and balance, repetition, texture, and focal points, together with the rule of thirds, lay the theoretical framework you need to create winter beauty in your garden. Hard landscaping, night lighting, trees and shrubs with provocative texture and bright color, and perennials and annuals with interesting seed heads are the design details that will bring that "special something" to your garden. Keep these things in mind when you choose hard landscaping, woody ornamentals (trees and shrubs), perennials, and annuals for your garden.

*A bird bath can be a
simple focal point.*
NORA BRYAN

KEY QUESTIONS FOR WINTER BEAUTY

One thing all prairie gardeners have in winter is time—long months to plan and dream. Even though a winter break is welcome, when you consider that the "break" can last more than six months, why not use it to plan a garden that looks good year-round? Winter is the perfect time to assess the overall design of your garden. It's also a lot easier to be objective without the blush of your favorite rose to distract you.

To decide what you think adds value to a winterscape, look outside and ask yourself:

- What do I see when I look out my windows? Is there anything to see?
- What parts of the garden are visible from the windows? What are the views and sight lines?
- Can I see out my windows at night or does looking out induce claustrophobia?
- Which rooms do I spend time in during winter? Am I in these rooms during the day or evening?
- Is my garden "flat" in winter, that is, does it lack vertical elements such as trees or a trellis?
- What are the main entrances for my family and guests? Are they inviting?
- What is the view when approaching my house?
- Does my garden have color beyond black and white?
- Do I have any evergreens?
- Are there any signs of life in winter? Are there birds in my garden?
- How deep is the snow in various parts of the yard? Are there snowdrifts that can be moved to cover more tender plants?
- Do I have any sculptural shrubs to build a winter vignette around?
- Which shrubs retain berries in winter? What color are the berries? Red? Orange? Yellow?
- Which annuals and perennials keep some color long after the first killing frost?
- Which plants have interesting bark?

*The ghostly gray color
and form of this clipped
cotoneaster (p. 106) contrasts
with the outward branching
pattern and gold-tipped foliage
of a savin juniper.*
BARBARA KAM

Three

Hardscapes, Ornamentation, and Lighting

WINTER IS A GREAT TIME TO ASSESS the "bones" of your garden, the major hard elements such as beds, paths, and patios, as well as how successfully you've integrated secondary elements such as ornamentation and lighting. For convenience, separate hard landscaping into horizontal and vertical design elements. There are practical and aesthetic considerations for using each in the winter garden.

Horizontal Design Elements

Horizontal elements like pathways, patios, and even garden beds are often lost under snow. However, aside from the necessity of keeping paths clear of snow, you can enhance these elements in ways that will add to your winter landscape.

Pathways

Major pathways should follow the most logical course, that is, the one most likely to be taken by family members and visitors. Make sure pathways are well delineated, so that even if snow blankets the garden, the route is easily picked out. Use low-voltage lighting fixtures or rows of pots, shrubs, or taller plants that hold their height and shape in winter to outline your paths. You don't want the letter carrier tripping over the garden gnome you got from Grandma, nor do you want the crowns of your tender plants scrunched under boot heels.

Snow melts more quickly from a dark-colored surface than a lighter one. Irregular pathways made of flagstones, large rocks, or loose material look great in summer, but make snow removal more difficult. You must decide how much effort you are willing to trade for a desired look.

Patios

At first glance, a patio doesn't warrant much winter attention. It is flat and often covered with snow. There are, however, some interesting uses for a patio in winter. Since patios are often adjacent to glass doors, improve your view from these doors by massing planters, pots, and garden ornaments in interesting ways (see Chapter Eight). Patios are also great places for bird feeders in winter because they are accessible for filling and viewing. Seed husks and spilled seeds are easily swept from the hard surface, rather than accumulating to molder or germinate later in your flowerbeds. Come summer, relocate the feeders back to their garden locales to avoid messy waste accumulation on patios.

THE ELEGANT VEGETABLE GARDEN

Even in the twenty-first century, we can learn a thing or two from the past. The parterre (literally French for "on the ground") is a flat garden that is arranged formally into geometric divisions; each part is outlined with small, clipped hedges or hard edging such as brick or stone. Although clipped boxwood hedges fall into the realm of fantasy in a winter prairie garden (English lavender or hyssop can substitute for those who simply must have a hedge), patterns made by sturdy landscape ties, bricks, or stone can be equally effective. Raised beds can also be enhanced in a parterre fashion. The spare elegance of a well-defined, patterned garden border is particularly sophisticated in winter.

Garden Bed Framing

Even the most artfully arranged perennial bed loses its appeal when frost defeats all vestiges of greenery. In winter there is limited plant evidence to differentiate your award-winning border from the neighbor's dog run. Still, your garden can hold winter charm long after cheerful flowers and elegant foliage have disappeared. For instance, you can edge informal beds with stones for a defined and graceful contoured perimeter; brickwork mosaics are perfect for formal beds. Vegetable or kitchen gardens can be transformed from rectangular lumps of dirt by designing them as parterres (see sidebar above).

Slightly undulating or raised beds hold more visual appeal than flat ones. Increase their appeal even more with natural materials, such as contorted driftwood and distinctive rocks. Raised or mounded beds look attractive under a blanket of snow. Rock gardens, in particular, possess all kinds of winter charm by virtue of the artful placement, textures, and colors of the chosen rock.

Vertical Design Elements

Careful choices in vertical elements can make the difference between a merely decent and a stunning garden in any season. Strong vertical elements are perhaps more important in winter than in any other season. If you are blessed with an abundance of trees and shrubs, most of the work may have been done for you. If not, there are still a number of things a prairie gardener can do to vertically enhance the winter garden.

Fences

Fences are usually constructed for privacy or to contain pets and children. In winter, fences play an additional role. They protect plants from the dehydrating bite of harsh winds, especially shrubs and small trees on the east or south side of a fence. Fences also trap valuable snow, which accumulates according to the placement of the fence relative to the prevailing winds. Strong winds may either physically pile up snow against the upwind side of a fence or may accumulate snow in drifts on the downwind side of a fence, several feet from the fence line. A bare area (a snow shadow) may develop on the immediate downwind side of a fence.

When stripped of their perennial clothes and deciduous leaves, fences reveal their angular nakedness. Soften their corners by grouping coniferous or densely branched shrubs in front of them. Add drama with the delicate tracery of vines. A dark-colored fence intensifies the image of snow-covered vines and shrubs. In the absence of snow, dark-colored vines embellish a somewhat lighter-colored fence or wall. A light-colored fence also highlights the color of evergreens, the bright stems of dogwood, or rose bushes thick with red hips. Finally, fences are great places to display attractive trellising or collections of some of your favorite objects. Who says that a fence can't have shelves? It will give you something to admire from your kitchen window.

Walls

Retaining walls or sloped rocky terraces can provide the perfect home for tiny treasures. Much-sought-after alpines and a variety of unusual plants, many of which might otherwise not be hardy here, can winter successfully

Eye-catching all year, a fence displaying collected objects or an artful trellis gathers even more charm with winter snows.
BARBARA KAM

in a well-planned rocky terrace. Even when alpines are blanketed by snow, individual rocks wear a scarf of white to provide visual relief.

Arbors and Trellises

Arbors and trellises are decorative in any season, but an arbor laden with the dried remains of vines takes on an especially lacy gracefulness after a light snowfall. In winter, the structures themselves come to the forefront. No longer hidden by greenery, the quality of their materials and design becomes a prominent feature in the winter garden, once again reminding gardeners that hard landscaping is not something to scrimp on.

Screens

In summer, screens are often used to provide shade or privacy in the garden. In winter, these screens can be relocated to protect tender shrubs and small trees from dehydrating winds. Place them so that your plants get maximum protection. Screens can be anything from creatively arranged temporary walls of shrub prunings, old fireplace screens, or artistic creations fashioned from branches of bamboo or willow.

Garden Ornamentation

Although designing the major horizontal and vertical elements of your garden required thoughtful planning and execution, now comes the fun part—decorating. Some gardeners may prefer a restrained and elegant winter garden, begging for just one special, carefully placed birdbath. Other gardeners may desire a more whimsical approach. Hang cheerfully decorated bird feeders. Rip the desiccated remains of summer's annuals out of pots or hanging baskets and fill them with conifer boughs, berried branches, and cut flowers (see Chapter Eight). And who says wreaths are just for Christmas? They can find homes on gates and fences or even laid on birdbaths. Do what you like—it's your garden!

Bring ornaments inside that seem unsuitable in a winter garden. There is something unsettling about naked garden cherubs in mid-winter, although gardeners with a sense of humor may prefer to outfit the cherubs with little toques and scarves to protect them from the elements. Experiment with relocating ornaments or statuary from their summer home to where you can see them better from indoors, unless you enjoy prowling through your garden in mid-winter. How about circling gnomes around a "campfire"?

White statuary placed in front of dark evergreens is a lovely study in contrast. Locate a birdbath near an electrical outlet and plug in a special heater that allows birds to enjoy a drink and a splash in winter. Sundials, obelisks, and fanciful plant stakes take on special drama as the low winter sun casts their long shadows over the snow.

Garden Lighting

Many of us never see our garden in mid-winter. We go to work when it's dark and return again in the dark. Our picture windows become black blocks on the wall. Yet we all know the enchantment of Christmas lights in our darkest month, so why not defy suburban conformity and consider garden lighting all winter, or maybe even all year? Inexpensive, low-voltage lighting kits are readily available. Strings of twinkle lights can be used year-round in the right places. Outdoor candles can add depth to the darkness and drama to special social occasions. Here are some options for lighting.

Low-voltage Lighting Sets

These easy-to-install kits usually contain a number of plastic or metal light fixtures that are staked into any soft ground. The light fixtures are attached—wherever the gardener wishes—to a length of power cord. The

The parterre design of these raised beds adds formal elegance to the garden year-round.
BARBARA KAM

cord that is exposed between the fixtures is then shallowly buried or hidden under paving stones. A transformer box, which changes the voltage from the household 110 volts to 12 volts, connects the string of fixtures to an outdoor wall socket. Although these sets are most commonly used for pathway lighting, you can place them anywhere in your garden that the power cord will reach. Take a tip from the experts and have a bit of extra cord available. This allows you to move the lights and make adjustments as plants grow.

Solar-powered Light Fixtures

These fixtures require no power outlet, as they have solar cells that use sunlight to power the bulbs. They can be placed anywhere in the garden where there is sufficient light. Unfortunately, these are rarely satisfactory for northern winter nights since the amount and angle of sun are much reduced at this time of year and the batteries do not get charged enough to function.

Floodlights

Inexpensive floodlights can be staked into the ground and plugged into a wall socket to highlight focal points in your garden, such as ornaments, conifers, and the trunks and branches of bare trees. There is some artistry and technique to effective spotlighting (see p. 23). Because floodlights are brighter than most garden lighting, use them sparingly on focal points.

Christmas Light Strings

Strings of clear lights can be enchanting additions to small trees or shrubs at any time of the year. Thread strings of clear twinkle lights around nicely shaped branches or trunks for a dramatic effect. The new net-style lights are an attractive alternative to tying burlap or rope around cedars and other conifers that need some protection from heavy snows. Use low-voltage, energy-efficient lights on evergreens to prevent undue heating that might lead to desiccation.

Professionally Installed Permanent Lights

In-ground, professionally installed light systems may be the way to go if you have a large property or you want something special. Since this type of system is difficult and expensive to change, make sure you know what it will look like before you start. Make a visual plan by stringing out temporary lights on extension cords in places where you think they will look good. Individually staked spotlights and utility lights also work well. Have willing family members or friends stand with flashlights in designated spots until you find the ones you like best. Don't forget the hot chocolate for your helpers once you have pinpointed your lighting locations.

EFFECTIVE SPOTLIGHTING

UPLIGHTING A spotlight aimed upward from the base of a deciduous tree accentuates the shape and texture of its trunk. Conifers are highlighted best when the light is aimed so that it brushes across the tips of their branches.

DOWNLIGHTING A light suspended over or from high up in a tree evokes the feeling of moonlight as it filters through the branches and casts shadows.

FEATURE LIGHTING To feature a piece of statuary, light it from two sides rather than from head on. For added drama, make one light brighter than the other.

ENLIGHTENED ADVICE

Although you should never allow your creativity to be overridden by self-appointed arbiters of good taste, there are some things about garden lighting to keep in mind when you embark on a lighting project.

NUMBER OF LIGHTS More is not always better. A single light, a few strategically arranged lights, or small strings of lights are probably sufficient. Avoid getting carried away. Your neighbors may not appreciate it, and you risk overloading circuits. Do not string more lights together than the manufacturer recommends.

AIMING LIGHTS Make sure lights are not aimed directly at your neighbor's or your own windows.

COLOR OF LIGHTS The color you choose is entirely personal, but clear lights will give your winter garden the most elegant look. Blue and green lights will emphasize its cold aspect, whereas yellow or red lights warm the scene. You decide what looks good. Just remember that if you use multiple colors, your neighbors may think you are too lazy to take down your Christmas lights.

TIMING Be careful when putting strings of lights on tree branches. Brittle, frozen branches break easily. Choose a day above freezing if you can.

TIMERS Even the most routine-oriented person finds an automatic timer to be a necessity. Set the timer so you can enjoy the lights from the moment you return home from work till bedtime. It saves on energy, too, because you won't neglect to turn them off.

Leave ornamentation out all year or relocate it for winter interest.
BARBARA KAM

The low winter sun creates shadow art.
NORA BRYAN

Even if unused most of the winter, a garden bench adds serenity to a scene.
BARBARA KAM

This easy-to-make ice candle votive welcomes guests.
NORA BRYAN

A string of clear lights and candles give depth to a dark winter night.
NORA BRYAN

CANDLE PROJECTS

Outdoor candle arrangements offer a dramatic welcome to party guests. They also give depth to the cold outdoors, which can be enjoyed by the people interacting inside.

FIRE IN ICE

What you need: an empty ice cream or similar-size pail, a soup can, marbles or rocks, a tea light, cranberries (optional)

What to do: Freeze about 5 cm (2 in.) of water in the pail.

Fill the soup can with rocks (for weight), and set it on top of the ice in the center of the pail. Add water to the pail up to the level of the soup can; add cranberries for color, if you wish, and then freeze the water in the pail. Remove the rocks from the soup can and fill it with boiling water to loosen the can from the ice. Remove the soup can, and then remove the ice block from the pail. Place a tea light in the hole left by the soup can.

PEONY RING CANDELABRA

What you need: a peony or tomato ring, baby food jars, craft wire, tea lights

What to do: Cut craft wire into 30-cm (12-in.) lengths. You'll need two pieces for each jar. Twist the centre of the wire around the neck of a jar and pull the ends up together. Repeat with another piece of wire, pulling the ends up on the opposite side of the jar. Twist the tops of the wires together and bend them to make a hanger. Push the peony ring into the ground or snow and hang the baby food jars at intervals. Add tea lights.

Four

Great Plants for Winter

OUR GARDENS ARE PLACES TO FIND COMFORT in time's passage and a continual reaffirmation of the life cycle. One of the glories of gardening in an area where the seasons change dramatically is the anticipation of what each season brings. We greet tulips warmly in spring, then bid them farewell for another year as their beauty fades and others take center stage. The passing weeks are filled with the wax and wane of each plant's glory, according to the calendar and the weather until, suddenly, fall asters, sedums, and changes in leaf color mark the end of the growing season.

Plants are important, even in winter. Conifers lend their color and shape year-round. Deciduous trees, no longer green and shady, show off their form, bark color, and texture. Even the vestiges of herbaceous perennials contribute surprising texture and color to the winter garden as they measure the passage of winter. In November or December, the monardas still poke their obstinate brown heads through the snow. In January, the crumbling of globe thistle seed heads reminds us that the new year has arrived. Their bent shapes are reflections of what was and suggestions of what will be again. When the waxwings come to clear mountain ash and crabapples of their fruit, we can be assured that spring is just around the corner.

The information in this chapter provides a way of thinking about plants, how they fit together, and the roles they play in the winterscape. Size, architectural form, bark color and texture, interesting seed heads, and vibrantly colored berries all contribute to the winter scene. Charts outlining specific plant features will help you to create your year-round garden.

Trees and Shrubs

You would be hard pressed to find a garden, however modest, in which trees and shrubs do not have a role. Even a newly built and landscaped property is bound to have its quota of trees and foundation shrubs; a property without them would seem unfinished even to a non-gardener.

Trees, shrubs, and some vines are aptly called woody ornamentals. "Woody" pertains to plants with stems that increase in width annually, have an outer layer of bark, and don't die down to the ground in winter. "Ornamental" describes why we have them. Woody ornamentals are the backbone of any garden and are fleshed out by leaves, flowers, annuals, and perennials during the growing season. Trees, shrubs, and vines add substance, beauty, privacy, and shade to our gardens. And, unlike annuals and perennials, which are generally either buried under snow, chopped down, or pulled out, woody ornamentals remain visible 365 days of the year.

Choosing Trees and Shrubs

Why do we select particular types of trees and shrubs? Often, it is for their floral display, their most transitory feature. Consider the beautiful, but ephemeral display of the lilac or forsythia; after the show of blooms, they fade into the background. If you want to have a beautiful garden year-round, however, give more attention and greater weight to other characteristics when you are deciding which tree or shrub to buy.

Choose woody ornamentals based on their performance and value every day of the year. Trees and shrubs are your most significant plant investment for the landscape, and fortunately, unlike things that lose their value over time, they appreciate with size and age. Although a small tree sold in a 15-liter (5-gallon) pot costs less than a balled and burlapped specimen with a trunk that is 5 cm (2 in.) in diameter, they are both more expensive to purchase than a typical perennial, so make your chosen tree earn its keep. Ask yourself if it does more than one of the following: flower in spring, have interesting leaf texture during summer, provide autumn color, present sculptural branching patterns and textured bark in winter, or attract winter birds with seeds, berries, or cover. The more seasons the plant works, the greater its contribution to your landscape.

Before deciding to add specific trees or shrubs to enhance your winterscape, take a dispassionate look at your existing landscape. Do you see balance and harmony within a solid framework? Is your framework as pleasing in winter as it is in summer? Given the cost, physical presence, and relatively long life span of woody ornamentals, you should not only select them carefully but also place those with winter interest where they are visible from

(a) Amur cherry
NORA BRYAN

(b) Crabapple
BARBARA KAM

Bark takes on special prominence in winter: (a) the shine of the horizontally exfoliating bark of Amur cherry; (b) the checkered texture of mature crabapple bark; (c) the white peeling bark of paper birch; (d) the copper glow of mountain ash bark; (e) the vertically peeling orange bark of the Scots pine.

(c) Paper birch
NORA BRYAN

(d) Mountain ash
NORA BRYAN

(e) Scots pine
BARBARA KAM

the warmth of your house and at entrances. In winter, the beauty of woody plants comes from their overall structure, from the fine details of their bark texture and color, and sometimes from their fruit, seeds, and leaves.

Hardy Stock: Tough Customers

Unlike inexpensive petunias and geraniums that can be tossed after months of summer pleasure without frustration, trees and shrubs are an investment, so always select those that are hardy in your area. Hardiness is defined as the ability of a plant to survive in a certain area. It is based on a number of factors, including minimum temperature tolerance; the ability to withstand fluctuating freeze-thaw cycles; the amount of moisture, snow cover, and wind that occurs in an area; soil texture (from clay to sand) and chemistry (pH); and the pests and diseases endemic to an area. These factors vary across the northern plains and, indeed, can vary within a city or even within a garden. Hardiness zones are a starting point for determining a plant's suitability. Neither the Canadian nor the American departments of agriculture use all the possible contributing factors when mapping hardiness zones; however, all factors are essential for assessing a plant's suitability and likely longevity.

Urban areas, due to warmth lost from buildings and traffic, create heat islands that can be a few degrees warmer than the surrounding environment. This temperature shift combined with the shelter from harsh winds provided by buildings may allow certain plants to survive the winter in the city, even though they would perish just a short drive away. As well, the harsh, dry conditions of the prairies often result in dwarfed versions of plants relative to other, more humid areas.

SCARY THOUGHTS ABOUT TENDER SHRUBS

Do you have some plants—challengingly known as "hardy once established"—that just need a few years of special care to get established? Many gardeners like to "push the zone," that is, to try to grow plants that would not survive winter without some coddling. It is up to each gardener to decide how much effort to put into overwintering plants, but it may well be worth some special effort. However, although each of us has our own sense of beauty, upright, burlapped evergreens can evoke frozen, mummified bodies awaiting spring burial, while leaf mounds over tea roses can suggest fresh burials. Granted, it is three dimensional and even apropos for Halloween, but does it meet your sense of beauty over the long, cold season?

If your garden permits, locate plants that require winter care where they are hidden from winter sight lines but still able to bring summer pleasure. If that's not possible, see Chapter Six for some more attractive options for winter protection.

Getting the Size Right

Remember, trees grow! That cute plant you got in the little black tub may someday take up half the yard. In this age of "instant" everything, it is easy to succumb to buying a tree that looks in proportion to your house now, but, in fact, will become a "growing" problem. The old saying "Live like you will die tomorrow, but garden as though you will live forever" encourages thoughtful plant selection. Always plan for the long term, even if you plan to move.

Before you buy any plant, but especially a tree, there are several things you should consider, the most critical of which are its mature height and spread. In the case of a tree, over time, you will have more shade in your yard, and if it has been placed improperly, you may also have issues with trunks and branches pressing against buildings and fences, tangling with overhead lines, and blocking entrances and views. In winter, the quality of your pruning job is on display—those summer hack jobs that were done to quickly lop off offending branches are very visible. Pollarded (topped) trees that looked lush and full during summer appear viciously mutilated in winter; weak twigs reach desperately in all directions from stumps, as if pleading against further disfigurement. It is a forlorn sight. With today's wide selection of cultivars, there is no need to buy an oversized tree and then continually prune it to size. With a right-sized tree, you will have little need to prune, beyond hedge maintenance and disease control.

A plant's dimensions also create a sense of scale with its surroundings and contribute to harmony or contrast. For example, too many spruce trees will tower over a bungalow, entirely hiding it from light and obstructing views. However, these same spruce trees may be entirely suitable as a windbreak in a rural area or as a feature plant in a more expansive suburban setting. Dwarf cultivars usually offer the same hardiness as the originals, plus they are the appropriate size for typical urban lots. If you cannot find the smaller versions, request them so that your local garden center knows the demand exists. Dwarf cultivars are often more expensive than their regular-size counterparts since they are slower growing and so must remain at the nursery longer to be of saleable size. However, with the increase in price, you get the benefit of less pruning and fewer potential problems. Just be prepared to be patient—because they start out smaller, it takes them longer to grow to the desired size.

The scale of acreages and rural properties permits grouping and interplanting of trees and shrubs in three layers—the canopy, understory,

*Textures change.
These crabapples
laced with hoar frost
will look different
another day.*
CALGARY ZOO

*Seed heads left standing,
such as those of this
Green Wizard rudbeckia
and Overdam feather
reed grass, add color and
movement to a winter
garden.*
NORA BRYAN

and groundcover—which mimic natural wooded areas. But within the structured confines of an urban lot, the use of trees is more singular, with massing occurring primarily with shrubs. The delineation between a small tree and a large shrub is subjective. In many smaller urban lots, large shrubs, such as Sutherland caragana, serve the same role as a small tree.

Winter Interest

Trees and shrubs take center stage in winter. Their architectural form, branching pattern, mass and visual balance, bark color and texture, and seed heads and berries enliven the winter garden.

Architectural Form In winter, we notice the form of our trees and shrubs. Naked elms line boulevards, reminding us of giant martini glasses. Columnar poplars stand at strict attention. Willows and crabapples become bent and gnarled in old age. From the weeping cascade of a grafted caragana to the open basket of a willow, the shapes of shrubs are also endlessly varied (see Tables 6 and 7).

The basic tree and shrub silhouettes either create unity in the landscape through repetition or create contrast through dissimilarity. They can be combined in many ways to provide balance, mass, and interest. Groupings of trees and shrubs undulate against the horizon, connecting land and sky. If you want to highlight a tree or shrub, have it stand alone or place it next to one of contrasting texture or color for tension and drama.

Branching Pattern Within the overall shape of a tree, its branching pattern adds another level of interest. Patterns range from strongly upright to horizontal. The direction of branches can point the eye to features or take the eye across the garden scene. For example, the vertical branching of the Sutherland caragana or the Swedish columnar aspen draws the eye skyward. The horizontal pattern of spruce boughs or creeping juniper spreads a scene outward. The pendulous branches of weeping birch and the arching branches of spring-blooming spirea lead our view on tangents. Weeping forms draw the eye downward toward water features or sculptures.

The size and arrangement of the leaf and flower buds on the branch add a further level of texture for the observant gardener. Tree forms and branching patterns create delicate shadow patterns in the snow, providing yet another thread to the winter tapestry.

Mass and Visual Balance If you want to achieve visual balance in the winterscape, you must first determine mass. The mass of a tree or shrub depends on the density of its branches and the size of its leaves. During summer, large-leaved plants generally appear denser than finer-leaved plants. The exception is fine-needled evergreens, which are denser and provide more visual weight than deciduous plants year-round, but particularly in winter. Density, of course, changes with the season. When densely clothed deciduous trees shed their leaves, they change from a solid lollipop shape to an open, branching form.

Densely branched trees and shrubs, such as cotoneaster, appear solid and lend visual weight to the winter garden. Their many closely spaced branches anchor the scene and also offer good backgrounds for other plants. In contrast, trees and shrubs that have an open (porous) branching pattern, such as dogwoods, appear light and airy. The long shadows of their branches glide quickly across the snow during the short daylight hours, creating silent performance art.

Bark Color and Texture Although tree trunks are visible during the summer, they are seldom appreciated, as they cannot compete with bright flowers demanding attention. In winter, however, a tree that appears semi-solid in summer becomes more transparent after it drops its leaves. This is when the tree reveals the color and texture of its bark, and just as human skin changes with age, so does the color and texture of bark.

Often, young stems have the smoothest bark and brightest color. Beyond neutral shades of gray and brown, bark colors include red, yellow, purple, orange, white, and green. The tones of this palette range from light to dark and serve to vary visual texture. Lighter-colored bark is generally perceived as more finely textured than darker-colored bark. Multiply these colors and tones with the various tree shapes, branch densities, and branching patterns and you'll see that there can be a great deal of variety in the winter landscape (see Table 4).

Place trees and shrubs where the subtleties of their winter color are shown off to full advantage. A tree or shrub with dark-colored bark is lost against a dark fence. Instead, place a paper birch, with its white bark, near a dark fence for great contrast. The red twigs of a Siberian dogwood lose vibrancy against a dark fence; a yellow-twigged variety is a better selection for that location. Alternatively, plant Siberian dogwood next to a light fence or an evergreen for a pleasing contrast.

The texture of the bark of a mature tree's trunk and branches is another element of winter interest. It may be smooth like mountain ash, peeling in horizontal strips like paper birch, shredding in vertical strips like the Scots pine, flaking like crabapple, or furrowed like bur oak and willow. Some trees such as aspen and chokecherries have horizontal markings, called lenticels, on their bark. The practical function of lenticels is air exchange, but we can appreciate them as additional decoration. Bark can also be shiny or dull, and spines, prickles, and thorns add to the mix. The shadows cast by oblique winter sun or night lighting give drama to bark texture and color.

Seed Heads and Berries As well as providing interesting bark and architectural form, some trees and shrubs retain colorful fruit or seed heads well into winter (see Table 8). These ornaments of nature add lively highlights to the usual restrained tones of winter. The pink-red tones of crabapples delight our eyes against the brilliant blue prairie sky and provide a tasty banquet for hungry winter birds. As a bonus, trees and shrubs that save their seeds and fruit for hungry birds mean there is less to clean up for you. Birds in the garden remind us that there is life in winter, fully engaging our senses with their color, movement, and chatter.

Coniferous Evergreens

Nothing says winter like a spruce laden with snow. Many people who garden in very warm climates envy us these distinctive trees. Although certain broad-leaved evergreens will survive in parts of the prairies, for hardiness purposes, this book focuses on conifers.

"Evergreen" is a misnomer on two counts. First, even conifers lose their needles after several years; that is why shedding from the inside branches is not cause for concern. Second, and more important to winterscaping, green is *not* a single color; there is a great deal of variety in hue and intensity. A coniferous evergreen can be blue-green (light or dark), gray-green (soft or bright), or even non-green, showing yellows, plums, oranges, or mauves (see Table 5).

Conifers come in a variety of forms, from widely prostrate to narrowly columnar. The shape that first comes to mind is the "Christmas tree," but the basic cone can be narrow and columnar like the Techny cedar and Sky Rocket Rocky Mountain juniper, or much broader like the Moonglow Rocky Mountain juniper and Montgomery blue spruce. There are also rounded forms like globe cedars, globe blue spruce, and mugo pines. The prostrate forms of many junipers lay flat against the ground or tumble over rocks and slopes, while vase-shaped forms, such as savin junipers, stand slightly taller. Some evergreens, such as a mature Scots pine or bristlecone pine, are irregularly shaped and look like giant bonsai. Weeping and creeping forms can be used as unusual focal points in a small garden. Finally, some evergreens, like mugos and Rocky Mountain junipers, can be pruned into topiary or bonsai shapes.

Although conifers usually lend visual weight to a garden, the amount varies. Both spruce and cedars are quite dense. Pines are more open and airy. If you put a mugo or cedar in a shadier situation, its branching habit opens wider. As you can see, the options for winter interest continue to grow.

Evergreens not only work well together, but also offer a great backdrop for shrubs and trees with colored twigs or interesting seed heads. Imagine how the red twigs of a dogwood shrub or the hips of a rose glow next to a mugo pine or how the burnished bark of a mountain ash gleams as it rises from a groundcover of junipers.

The Defiant Ones: Herbaceous Plants for a Winter Garden

Herbaceous perennials are those plants that return each year from the seemingly barren earth; although their aboveground parts die back in fall, their roots remain alive. Some perennials age gracefully and possess dignity, even after death, so instead of automatically crying "Off with their heads!" grant these plants a pardon. Indeed, gardeners are often unsure whether perennials should be cut back in fall or in spring. Although the English tradition is for fall cut-back, prairie gardeners can cut back the

Even the most exposed garden can delight with multihued tones and shapes of hardy shrubs. Here, a redleaf rose (p. 117) (foreground) and the burnished tones of a spirea (background) add color to the more subdued tones of horizontal juniper, mugo pine, and willows.
NORA BRYAN

TABLE 4: WINTER BARK COLOR OF SOME TREES AND SHRUBS

Common Name	Botanical Name
Red	
Japanese barberries (red-leafed cultivars)	*Berberis thunbergii* 'Cherry Bomb', 'Concorde', 'Rose Glow','Royal Burgundy', 'Royal Cloak'
Siberian coral (redtwig) dogwood cultivars	*Cornus alba* 'Sibirica', 'Argenteo-marginata', 'Bailhalo', 'Gouchaltii', 'Prairie Fire', 'Spaethii'
Red osier dogwood and cultivars	*Cornus sericea* and cultivars
Roses	*Rosa* x 'Thérèse Bugnet' , *R.* x 'Martin Frobisher'
Young stems of Marquette pussy willow	*Salix* x 'Marquette'
Orange	
Young stems of Siberian crabapples	*Malus baccata* and cultivars 'Columnaris' and 'Rosthern'
Scots pine	*Pinus sylvestris* and cultivars
Redstem willow	*Salix alba* 'Chermesina'
Flame willow	*Salix* 'Flame'
Bronze/Copper/Cinnamon	
Amur cherry	*Prunus maackii*
Pin cherry	*Prunus pensylvanica* and cultivars 'Mary Liss' and 'Stockton'
Mountain ash	*Sorbus decora, S. aucuparia*, and *S. americana*
Yellow	
Dogwood	*Cornus* 'Bud's Yellow', *C. sericea* 'Flaviramea' and 'White Gold'
Golden willow	*Salix alba* 'Vitellina'
White tones	
Paper birch when mature	*Betula papyrifera* and cultivar 'Chickadee'
European birch	*Betula pendula* and 'Gracilis', 'Fastigiata', 'Youngii' cultivars
Swedish columnar aspen	*Populus tremula* 'Erecta'
Tower poplar (green undertones)	*Populus* x *canescens* 'Tower'
Silver buffaloberry	*Shepherdia argentea*
Purplish brown	
River birch	*Betula nigra*
Purple-twigged dogwood	*Cornus alba* 'Kesselringii'
Rosybloom crabapples	*Malus* x *adstringens* cultivars, especially 'Thunderchild'
Nanking cherry	*Prunus tomentosa*
Young twigs of Schubert chokecherry	*Prunus virginiana* 'Schubert'
Young twigs of purpleleaf sandcherry	*Prunus* x *cistena*
Redleaf rose	*Rosa glauca*
Purple osier willow cultivars	*Salix purpurea* 'Gracilis' and 'Nana'
Japanese tree lilac	*Syringa reticulata* and cultivar 'Ivory Silk'

TABLE 5: SOME TREES AND SHRUBS WITH COLORFUL WINTER FOLIAGE

Color	Common Name	Botanical Name
Green	Mugo pines, cedars, savin junipers	*Pinus mugo, Thuja occidentalis, Juniperus sabina* 'Calgary Carpet'
Summer gold becomes muted orange	Motherlode juniper	*Juniperus horizontalis* 'Motherlode'
Summer color becomes plum-slate	Andorra, Bar Harbor, and Wilton's juniper	*Juniperus horizontalis* 'Andorra', 'Bar Harbor', 'Blue Rug' (syn. 'Wiltonii')
Silver-green	Gray Gleam and some Tolleson's weeping Rocky Mountain juniper	*Juniperus scopulorum* 'Gray Gleam' and 'Tolleson's Weeping'
Silver-blue	Blue Heaven, Medora, Moon Glow, Sky Rocket, some Tolleson's weeping, and Wichita blue Rocky Mountain juniper	*Juniperus scopulorum* 'Blue Heaven', 'Medora', 'Moon Glow', 'Sky Rocket', 'Tolleson's Weeping', 'Wichita Blue'
Blue tones	Blue Star juniper*, Blue Chip and Blue Prince juniper, Blue Danube, Tam, New Blue Tam savin junipers; blue spruce cultivars**	*Juniperus squamata* 'Blue Star'; *J. horizontalis* 'Blue Chip' and 'Blue Prince'; *J. sabina* 'Blue Danube', 'Tamariscifolia', and 'Tamariscifolia New Blue'; *Picea pungens* f. *glauca* cultivars
Yellow tips	Gold Coast and Aurea pfitzer junipers; Old Gold and Paul's Gold Chinese junipers	*Juniperus* x *pfitzeriana* (syn. *J.* x *media*) 'Gold Coast', 'Aurea', *J. chinensis* 'Old Gold', 'Paul's Gold'
Summer yellow tips become bronze	Canadian golden juniper	*J. communis* 'Depressa Aurea'
Summer green becomes purple-bronze	PJM rhododendron*	*Rhododendron* 'PJM'
Silver	Russian olive (some leaves remain)*	*Elaeagnus angustifolia*
Red	Barberry (some leaves remain)	*Berberis thunbergii* cultivars
Maroon-black	Turkestan burning bush (some leaves remain)	*Euonymus nanus* var. *turkestanicus*

* borderline hardy in the Chinook zone

** select them blue; they won't become bluer

TABLE 6: WEEPING TREES AND SHRUBS

Common Name	Botanical Name
Tolleson's weeping juniper	*Juniperus scopulorum* 'Tolleson's Weeping'
Weeping Norway spruce*	*Picea abies* 'Pendula', *P. abies* 'Inversa'
Weeping Colorado spruce	*Picea pungens* 'Pendula', *P. pungens* 'Glauca Pendula'
Weeping eastern white pine*	*Pinus strobus* 'Pendula'
Cutleaf weeping birch	*Betula pendula* 'Laciniata', 'Gracilis', 'Tristis'
Trost's dwarf weeping birch	*Betula pendula* 'Trost's Dwarf'
Young's weeping birch	*Betula pendula* 'Youngii'
European weeping birch	*Betula pendula*, *B. pendula* 'Fastigiata'
Weeping and Walker caragana	*Caragana arborescens* 'Walker', 'Pendula'
Weeping European larch	*Larix decidua* 'Pendula'
Weeping crabapple	*Malus* x 'Royal Beauty', 'Morning Princess', 'Red Jade'
Jumping pound pin cherry	*Prunus pensylvanica* 'Jumping Pound'
White weeping willow	*Salix alba* 'Tristis'
Weeping pussy willow*	*Salix caprea* 'Pendula'
Weeping mountain ash	*Sorbus aucuparia* 'Pendula'

* borderline hardy in the Chinook zone

TABLE 7: COLUMNAR TREES AND SHRUBS

Common Name	Botanical Name
Rocky Mountain juniper	*Juniperus scopulorum* 'Gray Gleam', 'Medora', 'Sky Rocket' and other cultivars
Columnar blue spruce	*Picea pungens* 'Fastigiata', 'Iseli Fastigiata'
Eastern white cedar	*Thuja occidentalis* 'Brandon', 'Techny'
Columnar eastern white pine*	*Pinus strobus* 'Fastigiata'
Columnar Scots pine	*Pinus sylvestris* 'Fastigiata'
European white birch	*Betula pendula* 'Fastigiata', 'Tristis'
Sutherland caragana	*Caragana arborescens* 'Sutherland'
Narrow common or European larch	*Larix decidua* 'Pendula'
Siberian columnar crabapple	*Malus baccata* 'Columnaris'
Swedish columnar aspen	*Populus tremula* 'Erecta'
Tower poplar	*Populus* x *canescens* 'Tower'
Columnar mountain ash	*Sorbus aucuparia* 'Fastigiata'

* borderline hardy in the Chinook zone

TABLE 8: TREES AND SHRUBS WITH INTERESTING BERRIES OR SEED HEADS

Common Name	Botanical Name
Amur or tatarian maple	*Acer tataricum* subsp. *ginnala*
Autumn Magic black chokeberry	*Aronia melanocarpa* 'Autumn Magic'
Hedge, European, and Peking cotoneaster	*Cotoneaster acutifolia; C. integerrimus,* and *C. lucidus*
Common sea buckthorn	*Hippophae rhamnoides*
Smooth hydrangea	*Hydrangea arborescens* 'Annabelle', 'Grandiflora'
Pee Gee hydrangea	*Hydrangea paniculata* 'Grandiflora'
Siberian columnar crabapple	*Malus baccata* 'Columnaris'
Rosthern ornamental crabapple	*Malus baccata* 'Rosthern'
Rosybloom crabapple	*Malus* x *adstringens* 'Almey', 'Garry', 'Kelsey', 'Radiant', 'Red Splendor', 'Rudolph', 'Selkirk', 'Thunderchild'
Smooth sumac*	*Rhus glabra* and *R. glabra* 'Laciniata'
Redleaf rose	*Rosa glauca*
Rugose rose and cultivars	*Rosa rugosa* and cultivars
Scots Briar and Altai roses	*Rosa spinosissima* and *R. spinosissima* 'Altaica'
Silver buffaloberry and cultivars	*Shepherdia argentea* and 'Goldeye' cultivar
American, European, and showy mountain ash trees and cultivars	*Sorbus americana, S. aucuparia, S. decora* and cultivars
Snowball viburnum	*Viburnum opulus* 'Sterile'
Highbush cranberry	*Viburnum trilobum, V. trilobum* 'Compactum' (syn. 'Bailey's Compact'), 'Garry Pink', 'Wentworth

* borderline hardy in the Chinook zone

Note: duration of berries and seed heads are impacted by presence of wildlife, harshness of the various seasons, and timing of frosts within a given year.

dead stalks of most herbaceous perennials any time between fall and spring, according to taste and enthusiasm.

Annuals are plants that complete their life cycle in a single year; next year's plants arise from seeds. These plants are almost synonymous with summer-long color, and it is hard to think of them as winter plants. As with many perennials, their winter charm lies in their seed heads.

Using Herbaceous Plants in a Winter Garden

A selection of standing plants in winter reinforces the vertical element that is so important to aesthetic views. To introduce this element into your winter garden, add sturdy plants with interesting seed heads to your summer border with an eye to future seasons. Otherwise, when your towering summer borders are cleaned up in the fall, all you may have left is a boring flat, brown space. Be forewarned, however. Some plants may put on a spectacular winter show one year, only to be flattened by heavy snows in the next. Fortunately, some plants get better as they get older, standing up to the elements to proudly show their winter glory. Every year offers a different display.

You may find that some plants with interesting texture or seed heads may not be sturdy enough to withstand winter snows in any year, but you can still enjoy them throughout the winter. Plants such as baby's breath, statice, sea holly, and globe thistle may be cut after they have dried and saved for winter containers. If cut at their peak, these flowers retain their color. Many other plants, often referred to as "everlastings," also retain their color if cut and dried at their prime (see p. 85).

Many grasses also retain their shape and height right through winter. The swaying plumes of rich golden feather reed grass will add height, color, and movement to your winter garden. For even more winter interest, the shorter blue fescue and blue oat grass retain their color and their radiating architectural patterns.

Evergreen Perennials

A pioneering spirit is called for when selecting evergreen herbaceous perennials for a prairie garden. Although they will never be a major feature of a winter garden, the few evergreen perennials that are available to the prairie gardener can add a curious dash of green here and there to an otherwise brown garden. Periwinkle and cliffgreen peek out from beneath fallen leaves in areas where snow cover is light. Evergreen rock garden plants, such as hen and chicks, bitterroot, and yucca, tucked into rocky crags seem to defy winter. When the glory of summer's color is long gone, these small evergreens can lift spirits on a bright, snowless winter day.

Vigorous Vines

An exuberance of lush vines seems unlikely in a place that is more at home with rippling plumes of grass. The number of vines that grow in our prairie gardens is relatively small, but they are beautiful year-round. The vertical tracery of stems intertwined over an arbor or clinging to a fence is rendered even more lacy and elegant by a sprinkling of snow. And it is not just the shapely architecture of vines that is entrancing. The feather-duster shape of clematis seed heads, the lanternlike pendants of the seed heads of hops, and the bright red berries of the nightshade vine are joyful sights all winter long.

TABLE 9: HERBACEOUS PLANTS WITH INTERESTING SEED HEADS

Winter Feature	Common Name	Botanical Name
Spherical or spiky seed heads	Ornamental onion	*Allium* spp.
	Globe thistle	*Echinops ritro*
	Sea holly	*Eryngium planum*
	Rudbeckia	*Rudbeckia fulgida*
Flat seed heads	Angelica	*Angelica gigas*
	Joe Pye weed	*Eupatorium purpureum*
Spiky seed heads	Blazing star	*Liatris spicata*
	Ligularia	*Ligularia* spp.
	Fleeceflower	*Persicaria affinis*
	Mullein	*Verbascum* spp.
Airy seed heads	Baby's breath	*Gypsophila paniculata*
	German statice	*Goniolimon tataricum*
	Sea lavender	*Limonium latifolium*
Knot, round, thimble, or buttonlike seed heads	Purple cone flower	*Echinacea purpurea*
	Poppy	*Papaver* spp.
	Siberian iris	*Iris sibirica*
	Globe centaurea	*Centaurea macrocephala*
Plumes	Astilbe	*Astilbe*
	Feather reed grass	*Calamagrostis* x *acutiflora*

TABLE 10: VINES FOR WINTER INTEREST

Winter Feature	Common Name	Botanical Name
Red and yellow seed heads	American bittersweet	*Celastrus scandens*
Architectural form, feathery seed heads	Clematis	*Clematis macropetala* *C. tangutica*
Architectural form, lanternlike seed heads	Common hops	*Humulus lupulus*
Architectural form, red berries	Climbing nightshade	*Solanum dulcamara*
Architectural form of mature plants	Virginia creeper; Engelmann ivy	*Parthenocissus quinquefolia* and cultivar 'Engelmannii'

TABLE II: EVERGREEN GROUNDCOVERS FOR WINTER INTEREST

Common Name	Botanical Name
Peachleaf bellflower	*Campanula persicifolia*
Cheddar pinks	*Dianthus gratianopolitanus* cultivars
Cliffgreen	*Paxistima canbyi*
Bitterroot	*Lewisia cotyledon*
Creeping mahonia	*Mahonia repens*
Hen and chicks	*Sempervivum* x
Lesser periwinkle	*Vinca minor*

THE RISK OF RUST

Many of the plants that partner well for winter—the oranges or reds of berries on plants of the *Rosaceae* family and the greens of junipers—are also alternate hosts for various species of *Gymnosporangium* fungi, which cause diseases commonly known as cedar-apple rusts. These rusts infect junipers, particularly Rocky Mountain junipers, apples, crabapples, hawthorns, saskatoons or serviceberries, pears, gooseberries, mountain ash, and cotoneasters, among other plants. On deciduous plants, the rust looks like orange (rust) spots. On evergreens, the symptoms depend on the rust species. For example, it looks like brown galls or orange gelatinous spots on junipers.

Fungi produce vast numbers of spores that can spread by water, wind, pruning equipment, and birds. Once a spore finds a suitable host, it requires a warm, humid environment for germination. This is one time we can be thankful that the combination of warmth and humidity are not common to most of the prairies. Rust generally does not kill a plant but can weaken it, cause leaf drop, stunting, branch die-back, and deformed fruit.

Many publications recommend removing the offending junipers to reduce the risk of rust, but these publications usually pertain to managing orchards and reducing economic loss from fruit damage. In an urban lot, if you remove your juniper, there is no guarantee that your neighbor will follow suit. Nor can you prevent rain, wind, bugs, and birds from carrying spores from an infected plant down the street onto your treasures. The best control is to select relatively rust-resistant cultivars, prune infected parts, and clean up infected debris. If the rust is mild on a deciduous plant, pull off the offending leaves and dispose of them, but don't compost them.

*Even without snow, this terraced garden
highlights some of winter's colors. The
globe blue spruce (*Picea pungens *f.* glauca
*'Globosa') (p. 132) repeats the color of the
horizontal Blue Rug juniper in the foreground
and both contrast nicely with the cinnamon
clipped spirea hedge (p. 125) and green
bristlecone pine. Calgary Carpet juniper
(*Juniperus sabina *'Calgary Carpet') (p. 129)
contributes a fresh green, while the soft warm
tones of flame grass and oat grass complete
the scene.*

NORA BRYAN

Putting It All Together—
Great Plant Groupings

NOW THAT YOU'VE HAD A LOOK AT YOUR GARDEN and been intrigued by the possibilities, it's time to create your own winterscape. Use the rule of thirds—one-third evergreens, one-third deciduous trees and shrubs, and one-third annuals and perennials—as a guideline for assembling great plant groupings to admire from your favorite window. Think about balance and harmony, repetition, contrast, and focal points as you plan your groupings (see Chapter Two). When you're done, add some lighting and ornamentation and your scene will delight both day and night.

Think contrasts when planning for shrubs and trees. They are the stars of the winter garden, with their varied shapes, colors, and textures. For example, use conifers to highlight the red and orange tones of deciduous fruit and bark. Place woody ornamentals with light bark against dark backgrounds and and those with dark bark in lighter settings. Coordinate cool blue-toned conifers with silver perennials and bark to contrast with beige expanses of lawn devoid of snow. Group various deciduous woody ornamentals, grasses, and perennials to warm the frosty white snow. Here are some more ideas to help you along.

Winter Wonder

Given the vast expanse of time between the final fading of fall asters and the appearance of the first plucky spring bulbs, the idea of creating a garden bed that's especially bold in winter makes sense. An American highbush cranberry or mountain ash fronted by vase-shaped savin junipers that are, in turn, edged with tall sedums may seem modest in summer. In winter, however, the arching juniper branches wear ermine scarves of snow that provide an elegant underpinning for the glowing, jewel-like berries of the mountain ash or cranberry, while the sedums wear sparkling snow tiaras.

To add to this winter scene, move summer statuary or a birdbath amidst the junipers for a focal point. You have no statuary? Try tipping and stacking some terra-cotta pots or creating a stone inukshuk in front of the junipers for a simple yet regal winter arrangement. Add glow to the night by running twinkle lights through the shrubs or by spotlighting the statuary.

Year-round Beauty

The often dull, brown season from October until the snows of January really start to fly can be a challenge for a prairie gardener. One solution is to choose plants that lend pleasing color and texture with or without a gentle mantle of snow. For instance, imagine the arching, pale pink-orange leaves of flame grass rising like a fountain from behind a short Goldmound spirea hedge. In front of the hedge lies an emerald Calgary Carpet juniper. Between the juniper's branches, straw-colored drumsticks of blue allium reach out to play against the winter cinnamon of the spirea hedge. At the end of the hedge, next to the juniper, sits a large urchin of blue oat grass painted a tow color by the brush of autumn winds. The light, porous grass spikes contrast dramatically with the dark density of the spirea and juniper.

This combination also provides a succession of interest during the growing season. First come the blue-flowered alliums that then turn into attractive seed heads. Later the spireas bloom pink and the air is filled with the buzzing of bees. The luminous yellow of the Goldmound spirea plays well with the steely blue of the oat grass. As an added advantage, this is a low-maintenance combination, requiring only a quick spring cleanup.

Rocky Revelations

A background of mixed conifers and dogwoods makes a rocky foreground populated with plants that retain great shape and rich color through winter look even better. Yucca presents a dramatic green burst year-round, through all but the deepest snow cover. The spiky dried seed heads of phlomis poke through light snowfalls. For a similar effect, you can substitute tufts of blue fescue or larger blue oat grass for the yucca and liatris or persicaria for the phlomis. Add a soft curve of silvered driftwood to contrast with the spiky yucca and blue spruce. And, as the winter progresses, the undulations of deeper snow cover over the rocks will add a further dimension of texture.

Small plants like hen and chicks and thyme endear themselves in early winter before snow covers the scene. These short plants, which often remain green while days are warm and nights are below freezing, create a rich tapestry with fallen gold leaves interwoven with bent stems of brown and silver plant remains. The richness of the brocade intensifies when touched by rime. But be sure to admire these diminutive beauties under the sunny, blue skies of early winter, as they are likely to be blanketed with snow from January to March.

Perennial Foils

Planting tall, later-blooming perennials to provide height that would otherwise have to be achieved with shrubs is a good way to maximize your plant choices, especially if you have a small garden. Because these perennials start off slowly in spring, you can create other looks in spring and summer with shorter plants and spring bulbs.

A medium-size mugo pine is an attractive four-season foil for a revolving array of perennials. To go from fall right through winter in an elegant fashion, place tall, late-blooming perennials such as feather reed grass and rudbeckia in front of the mugo pine. This gold and bronze combination not only glows under the blue prairie sky but also illustrates the effective use of height layering and textural contrast. You can substitute echinacea or teasel for the rudbeckia and panicum for the feather reed grass.

A medium-size blue spruce cultivar teamed with globe thistle or sea holly results in a similar composition but in cooler blue and silver tones. Feather reed grass would add a pleasing contrast in texture and tone to this composition. Repeat the silver-blue theme with blue oat grass or blue fescue in the foreground. Place perennials with pale, delicate structures, such as baby's breath, statice, or Russian sage, against dark conifers to highlight their color and details.

Shining Shrubberies

You can make any number of fantastic groupings by taking advantage of the great variety of shapes, sizes, and colors of small and dwarf trees and shrubs. The blues of spruce and juniper always complement the mid-green of a pine or a cedar. A globe spruce anchors a swath of arching savin junipers. A predominance of conifers will make a scene permanent and somewhat heavy. To lighten this scene and to add seasonal variation, incorporate some deciduous shrubs and trees.

Height, density, and color are other important elements of groupings. Columnar crabapples or Swedish columnar aspen add narrow, spare height. The open baskets of dogwoods or willows lend grace. A densely branched cotoneaster provides an ethereal orb of silvery gray. Spirea imparts a rich brown color that glows under a bright sun. The fiery stems of Siberian coral dogwoods deliver a punch of contrasting color against rich green pines. Classic combinations of red and green seem to suit the winter landscape, but lesser-used combinations can be just as vivid. Team a blue spruce with yellow-twigged dogwoods or a gold-stemmed willow for sophisticated variation.

For larger properties, a great way to have a carefree scene that works in any season is to group small or medium-size trees and shrubs. For example, a medium-size blue spruce cultivar such as 'Hoopsii' or 'Fat Albert' contrasts well with the mid-green of a mugo pine. Repeat the blue tones with a creeping blue spruce. The white bark of a columnar birch adds height and provides contrast with the darker spruce. Large rocks anchor the scene. If these plants are too large for your garden space, scale down by grouping Rocky Mountain juniper, dwarf mugo pine, and the narrower Chickadee birch. All of these low-

The remains of Rudbeckia hirta 'Indian Summer' (p. 162) hold their color under a frosty blue prairie sky to complement feather reed grass and a pine.
NORA BRYAN

maintenance trees and shrubs shine in winter.

You may already have great groupings in your garden. If you're not sure, though, leave your yard clean-up until spring and have a serious look at your garden groupings over the winter. This is the best way to decide what works for you and what doesn't.

A grouping of various colored conifers, deciduous trees or shrubs, and rocks creates a year-round focal point. In this grouping, a small creeping spruce contrasts with a mugo pine. Birch and taller blue spruce add height and additional color contrast.
NORA BRYAN

Blue spruce, mugo pine, and dogwoods provide a backdrop for yucca and the stout remains of other rock garden plants.
NORA BRYAN

ATTRACTIVE ASSOCIATES

- Feather reed grass (*Calamagrostis* x *acutiflora*) or purple moor grass (*Molinia caerulea* cultivars) in front of Joe Pye weed (*Eupatorium* spp.)
- Russian sage (*Perovskia atriplicifolia* cultivars), Coronation Gold yarrow (*Achillea* 'Coronation Gold'), and blue oat grass (*Helictotrichon sempervirens*)
- Skinner's golden brome grass (*Bromus inermis* 'Skinner's Gold') or lyme grass (*Elymus arenarius*)
- Echinacea (*Echinacea purpurea*) with blue fescue (*Festuca glauca*)
- Liatris (*Liatris spicata*) with showy stonecrop (*Sedum spectabile*)
- Echinacea (*Echinacea purpurea*) fronted by Kobold liatris (*Liatris spicata* 'Kobold')
- Cedar (*Thuja occidentalis*), Siberian dogwood (*Cornus alba* 'Sibirica'), and purple moor grass (*Molinia caerulea*)
- Redleaf rose (*Rosa glauca*) and mugo pine (*Pinus mugo* var. *mugo*)
- Redleaf rose (*Rosa glauca*) and Calgary Carpet juniper (*Juniperus sabina* 'Calgary Carpet')
- Feather reed grass (*Calamagrostis* x *acutiflora*) behind a round spirea (*Spiraea* x *bumalda*)
- Dwarf mugo pine (*Pinus mugo* var. *pumilio*) and Amur cherry (*Prunus maackii*)
- Mountain ash (*Sorbus* spp.) and creeping juniper (*Juniperus horizontalis* spp.)
- German statice (*Goniolimon tataricum*) edging a crabapple (*Malus* x *adstringens* cultivars)

Six

Preparing for Winter

YOUR NEIGHBORS HAVE MOWED THEIR LAWN to the prescribed height and given the grass its fall feeding. All of their dried plant remains have been duly amputated and the earth raked bare of leaves and debris. You, in contrast, procrastinate too long. The freezing rain that came down on the day you chose to do your fall cleanup persuades you to stay indoors and read a good book. Eventually, snow covers your neglected garden and your guilty sensations subside. You notice a few coneflower stems sticking out of the snow; they look quite charming and the birds are keen on them. Come spring, when you finally get around to raking off fall's leaves, you discover to your delight that the mini-roses you assumed were cute annuals have survived the winter.

Gardening tradition in more temperate climates stresses the importance of fall yard maintenance, and often with good reason. You want to prevent fungi and diseases from establishing. In gardens that remain mostly green all year, cutting back plants in fall keeps up appearances and makes the garden look well tended. But prairie gardens in winter are a world away from these verdant gardens. So, if you have failed again to make everything shipshape by freeze-up, do not despair. Such seeming neglect can actually be a virtue, both in terms of good garden practices and aesthetics, and it is a boon to those gardeners who prefer not to do the same work twice.

Why do most of us go to great lengths to prepare our gardens for winter? Maybe our urge to tidy comes from the puritanical notion that

Don't be too hasty with the clippers. Late-blooming plants such as mullein and sea holly not only add punch to the fall garden but retain interest through to spring.
NORA BRYAN

cleanliness is next to godliness. After all, aren't most gardeners trying to exert a bit of control over their own personal Garden of Eden? Maybe we do it because the "experts" tell us we should. As one gardener puts it, tidying the garden in fall is like cleaning up right after a party rather than waiting for the dirt to settle.

When it comes to gardening, some tasks can be safely ignored or left until spring, although others definitely should be looked after in the fall to help plants tough out the winter season. Here are some suggestions to help you decide what needs to be done in the fall and what can be left till spring.

Perennial and Mixed Borders

After perennial plants have died back, they will eventually have to be cut down to keep the garden tidy. Tradition compels you to chop back perennials in the fall, leaving a short length of stem to catch snow, yet you know you'll be back out there come spring cutting them back further still. Save yourself some work and do it all in the spring. Really, wouldn't you rather be doing something fun in fall, like designing a winter arrangement? Two other advantages to a spring cleanup are that plant tops are more easily removed in spring—a quick tug is usually all it takes—and old plant debris helps mark the spot for plants that are "late-emergers."

Most plants can be left intact to provide winter interest or protection for the underlying crown of the plant. Many plants die well, leaving interesting seed heads to charm us and to provide food for overwintering birds. This is how nature does it, and it works. You may, however, want to cut back certain plants in fall to prevent rampant self-seeding or the spread of fungus and disease. When you cut stems back, leave several centimeters (a few inches) of stalk to trap leaves and snow.

Keeping plants intact may result in volunteer plants next spring. However, leaving seed heads does not add significantly to a gardener's "to-do" list; it shifts the timing of the work. You trade the benefit of winter beauty and less fall clean-up for a bit more work in summer. In spring and early summer, a quick weekly scuffle with a cultivator will knock out newly germinated seedlings. No need to pull them or pick them up, the seedlings will quickly brown to blend with your soil or mulch. You don't even have to bend over; it's a low maintenance way to deal with the results of leaving plants standing over winter. If the concept of leaving most plants standing through winter is initially scary, clean up the areas outside your winter sight lines.

Rather than raking all the leaves from your perennial beds—only to put down compost or winter mulch later—why not let leaves accumulate naturally, as they do in a forest? This saves you from raking twice, once in the fall and once in spring, and the natural decay of leaves provides future nourishment for the trees they came from and the other plants that share their space. The leaves also keep in valuable moisture and provide important winter mulch, which protects tender plant crowns and hibernating, pest-eating ladybugs from unseasonable temperature fluctuations. Some gardeners are concerned about letting poplar leaves remain on garden beds over winter because the leaves have a tendency to lie flat, which may prevent water and air from getting through. Others use poplar leaves with impunity. It is probably best to take large poplar leaves and chop/shred them with a lawnmower first, before spreading them on garden beds.

Winter Mulch

Mother nature protects the delicate crowns of perennials and evergreen groundcovers with snow cover and fallen leaves. This light and airy mulch may be all that is needed in most cases. However, in the Chinook belt or where winter winds repeatedly rip off snow cover, and for borderline-hardy perennials or evergreen deciduous plants and tender shrubs, nature may need a helping hand. Apply a winter mulch if you do not use an all-season mulch, or top up your all-season mulch in fall.

Winter mulch moderates soil temperature fluctuations and thus protects against frost-heaving during alternating freeze-thaw cycles; prevents soil from warming up too soon in spring, or during unseasonably warm spells in winter; and protects evergreen groundcovers from desiccating winds. Mulches do not, as is sometimes believed, keep the soil from freezing. Soil will always freeze on the northern prairies.

Winter mulch is applied thickly, after solid freeze-up, over the crowns of garden plants and may be heaped to completely cover small tender shrubs. Some gardeners take their cue from nature and just allow leaves to accumulate naturally as they fall from trees. Other gardeners bag their leaves and stack the bags over beds containing borderline-hardy plants—very neat and saves lots of work in spring, but is not particularly attractive. Straw has very good insulating properties but tends to get messy, and may contain weed seeds. Even conifer boughs scavenged from discarded Christmas trees work well.

HOW PLANTS PREPARE FOR WINTER

Winter dormancy is an important part of northern plant survival, so don't begrudge your plants their winter disappearing act. After rising from the cold earth in May to reach full flowering splendor in a few short months, they deserve a breather. Here is how they prepare for winter.

WINTER DORMANCY

Dormancy is triggered in a plant by a combination of chilling period, photoperiod (day length), and cultural conditions, such as drought stress. Northern plants need a gradual chilling period and a gradual warming period to trigger strong new growth in spring. These prescribed periods are programmed by a plant's native area, which is why a plant performs best in climates that are closest to that of its native area.

Developing buds of woody plants and bulb tunics, the paperlike sheath that protects bulbs, are, in fact, tight covers that protect the plant's embryonic tissue. These magical covers are infused with hormones that prevent growth; they also contain a balanced concentration of water to resist both frost damage and dehydration.

To prepare for dormancy, hardy shrubs and trees pull water from their trunk and stem cells, leaving behind concentrated fluids that act like antifreeze inside the cell. The water is isolated outside the cell until the plant needs it again in spring. Non-hardy plants are unable to do this; their water-filled cells shatter when they freeze.

A QUICK START

Conifers have an overwintering strategy that allows them to be ready and waiting to resume growth when the warmth of spring returns. To make the most of a growing season that may last less than half a year, many conifers begin photosynthesis as soon as the temperature rises above freezing. Their slim, tough needles are designed to resist desiccation and shed snow easily. Flexible branches that are layered like shingles support snow efficiently and shed excess snow easily. Some deciduous trees such as aspens have quick-start tricks as well. Aspens are capable of photosynthesizing through their greenish bark, which contains chlorophyll. Lens-shaped lenticels on their trunk allow gas transfer before leaves develop.

DUCKING WINTER

Many northern plants retreat underground during winter. Herbaceous perennials die back to their crown at ground level. Their roots have stored nutrients to start new growth in spring.

SELF-SACRIFICE

Annual plants do not survive winter; instead, they self-sow, having set lots of seed. Allow annuals and biennials (plants that die after the second year) to set seed if you want them to return each year.

PLANTS TO CUT BACK IN FALL

Although many plants can be left standing through winter, others may be cut back in fall to prevent over-exuberant seeding, disease, or just plain "ickiness" come spring. Bearded iris and peonies are among those plants that are best cut back in fall to prevent possible spread of fungi. Otherwise it is really up to you to identify candidates for fall versus spring clean-up. To help you decide, keep notes on what you dislike to clean up in spring.

BEYOND THE BLUE TARP

Instead of the usual piles of leaves held down with old carpet scraps or a tarp to cover your delicate beauties, such as tender roses and other borderline plants, indulge your creative fantasies to come up with more attractive cover-ups. Clearly, form follows function, but there is always room for beauty.

DECORATED BOXES

Instead of rose huts, make your own boxes out of 5-cm (2-in.) Styrofoam™ insulation panels, held together with waterproof carpenter's glue. Decorate your boxes using waterproof markers or paints.

STICK PYRAMIDS AND OBELISKS

Pile leaves over tender shrubs and arrange willow poles (or even sturdy conifer boughs) teepee fashion over top. Tie the tops of the poles with hemp rope or shock cords. Decorate with a ribbon or raffia bow.

Inventive coverings for tender shrubs, such as this expandable obelisk, have more charm than Styrofoam™ rose huts. BARBARA KAM

Trees and Shrubs

Keep trees well watered in autumn, until the leaves turn color. Frozen ground and drying winter winds can stress a tree that goes into winter dehydrated.

Conifers especially need to have sufficient water stored in their needles and trunk to tide them through mild spells in winter because they photosynthesize and lose water through transpiration whenever the temperature is above freezing. They should not, however, be drowned, which can happen in clay soil that retains water. Young conifers, cedars, firs, and Norway spruce should definitely be watered until freeze-up, but even drought-tolerant conifers such as pine, Colorado spruce, and juniper benefit from additional water during an exceptionally dry fall.

Don't prune trees and shrubs at this time of year. Pruning stimulates growth so is normally done in late winter or early spring when plants are dormant. Birch and maple trees are the exception; they are pruned in late summer after their sap has stopped running. However, it is okay to harvest some healthy dogwood and evergreen branches in fall for winter containers. Also, dead or damaged branches that might crack under the weight of winter snow or freezing rain should be removed in early fall. Remember that frozen branches are brittle, and attempts to remove dangling limbs after freeze up may result in damage to other branches.

In general, on the prairies, avoid using strong nitrogen fertilizer in fall. Nitrogen stimulates new top growth, and woody plants should be hardening-off for winter. Although shrubs such as roses benefit from regular fertilizing in the growing season, you should stop fertilizing them about six weeks before the first hard frost. During early autumn, as leaves change color, the soil is still warm and trees put on root growth as they prepare for winter. Some people recommend a winterizing fertilizer high in phosphorous and potassium for trees. If you choose to try to protect borderline-hardy trees with a fall fertilization, confirm with your arborist that the percentage of nitrogen is significantly less than the phosphorous or potassium, and ideally no more than 10 per cent.

Shrubby columnar conifers such as juniper and cedar are sometimes wrapped in burlap to prevent their branches from being torn off under heavy snows. In areas where snowfall is rarely heavy, or if shrubs are under protective eaves, wrapping is unnecessary. If you do use wrapping, don't bind your shrubs so tightly that air circulation between branches is impeded. There are also some attractive alternatives to burlap wrapping (see pp. 60–61) that you may want to investigate.

Young trees with thin bark may suffer sunscald or frost-cracking, particularly if bark on the southwest side of the trunk is exposed. Bark on this side heats up dramatically on sunny days, only to freeze rapidly at night. Over time, this process may blister the bark, which may eventually split, leaving an open wound. To guard against this, loosely wrap trunks of young trees with special tree wrap. Alternatively, try planting shrubbery or placing screens on the southwest side of young trees so you can still enjoy their beautiful bark in winter.

Another reason to wrap trunks is to prevent feeding damage by rodents and hares, although older trees are less susceptible to this problem. Be sure to remove the wrapping in spring.

If you choose trees and shrubs that are suitable for our climate and plant them where they will perform best, then you won't have to wrap them in winter. This means you will be able to enjoy their appearance year-round. Caragana, for instance, is ideal for dry, windy sites. Hardy shrub roses do best where they get full sun and some natural protection from winter's worst moods. When given the conditions they prefer, neither requires winter protection.

If, however, you find a borderline-hardy shrub you can't do without, then give it some extra winter protection. Many gardeners simply pile dry leaves or straw over their tender charges and drape netting, tarps, or old scraps of carpet on top. The shrub may find this satisfactory, but it is not very attractive to look at. Little rows of Styrofoam™ "rose huts" are no more charming. The situation calls for some creativity. Why not dress up your tender shrub hideaway in elegant or whimsical ways? Wouldn't Styrofoam™ covers disguised as a row of charming "cottages" or interesting packages be more appealing? Perhaps your children's artistic streaks could be put to better use on the rose huts than on your kitchen walls (see p. 56 for alternatives).

Desiccation in Evergreens

On the prairies, the most limiting factor for the survival of evergreens, particularly cedar, fir, and broadleaf evergreens, is winter desiccation (drying). This is because plants that keep their leaves in winter continue to photosynthesize during warm, sunny days, using water that they stored in their leaves, stems, and roots before the ground froze. A plant with insufficient water reserves dehydrates to the point that its leaves brown and die. There are several ways to combat desiccation.

Select Prairie-hardy Evergreens Spruce, pine, and junipers are good choices.

Put Plants in the Right Spot For example, cedars, firs, and dwarf Norway spruce are best on the north or east side of a house or in the shelter of other shrubs, out of the wind and direct winter sun. Give the plants a thorough soaking in late autumn.

If the Soil Thaws and Is Dry, Water It There is much debate about the value of watering evergreens in winter. If you live in an area where freeze-thaw cycles are quite common, it may help to water cedars, firs, and newly planted trees if the ground thaws. There is no point in watering frozen ground. Mature junipers, pines, and spruce are likely tough enough to survive without extra water. Avoid overwatering conifers, though, particularly those in clay soil. Their roots may rot if they "wake up" to a cold, mucky bog in spring.

Mulch the Root Area A year-round protective layer of bark chips, shredded leaves, or other organic material around the base of the plant, to at least the drip-line, helps conserve water. The insulating effect of the mulch layer moderates changes in soil temperature and delays freeze-up, allowing a longer period of water uptake by the roots in the fall. Any available snow can be put to good use by piling it gently around young conifers.

Use Windbreaks, Wrapping, or Screens Windbreaks, wrapping, or screens can also be used to protect plants from drying winds. As trees and shrubs become established, this type of protection may not be required. Ultimately, though, wrapping defeats the purpose of having an "evergreen" in winter and indicates that perhaps the plant was not situated properly in the first place.

What About Anti-transpirants?

Transpiration is the evaporation of water through the pores (stomata) of leaves and stems. This natural phenomenon accompanies photo-synthesis, which evergreens continue to undergo whenever temperatures are above freezing. Transpiration also cools plants, like perspiration cools our bodies. Most anti-transpirants (also known as anti-desiccants) act to block water loss physically by coating the leaf with latex, wax, acrylic, or resins. The substance clogs the stomata where water exits the leaf. Solar reflectors are another type of anti-transpirant; they keep the leaf cooler by reflecting sunlight, so there is less need for transpiration.

The use of anti-transpirants is sometimes recommended to prevent winter drying and subsequent browning of living evergreens, as well as the browning of Christmas trees, wreaths, and cut flowers, and the dehydration of stored bulbs. Although they may be useful for some of these purposes, the jury appears split on the benefits of anti-transpirants for preventing winter browning on living plants, particularly in our climate.

Some publications recommend these products for live evergreens, especially broad-leaved ones. Others argue that blocking the stomata of living plants interferes with their function. On a sunny day, the plants will be unable to transpire and thereby cool themselves, possibly causing cell damage due to overheating. Further, if water is prevented from leaving the leaf, the gas exchange that is essential to plant health is impeded. Plants evolved to deal with trade-offs between photosynthesis and transpiration long before there were anti-transpirants.

As well, anti-transpirants may not be appropriate for use on the northern prairies. For example, the label of one popular product reads, "Spray in late fall when temperature is above 40°F [4.4°C] ... Avoid using on cedar, juniper, cypress and arborvitae where deep freezing may occur within two months of application." Clearly, the product will not be of much value where temperatures can plunge dramatically in a matter of days. If you are going to purchase a product to reduce transpiration on living plants, read the label first.

THE JAPANESE WAY: SUPPORTING SNOW-LADEN BRANCHES

An art form of propping up snow-laden boughs has been developed in the Kenrokuen Garden in Kanazawa, Japan. The Karasaki pines in this garden have a very large spread and their boughs are supported by a *ringo-tsuri*, a maypole-like support structure with the tall pole positioned near the trunk. Ropes hanging from the top of the pole are fastened to the branches to support them. For shrubs, the *shibori* technique is used; a rope is tied about the shrub to gather the branches and protect them from the weight of winter snow. The simple beauty of these elegant supports is inspiring and may be used to similar advantage in prairie winter gardens.

ARTFUL SCREENS

Exposed shrubbery benefits from screening on its windward side to reduce the dehydrating effect of relentless winter wind. Screens can be as simple as brush piles or as elaborate as artful creations of willow or lattice. A screen with holes is better than a solid wall, however. A solid wall forces wind up and over the wall, causing it to rush over the downwind side and making the problem of dehydration even worse. The usual squares of burlap stapled to a frame do the trick, but these can be improved upon by some simple and artful substitutions. For example:

• Use old fireplace screens.

• Relocate an iron or willow screen that you use during summer for privacy to the windward side of cedars.

• If you must use burlap, paint a picture on it, so it becomes artwork framed by its support posts, rather than a brown block.

Lawns

The traditional advice to cut the lawn slightly shorter than normal for winter is solid; long grass may develop snow mold. This fungus appears as a grayish film on the lawn in spring. A lush lawn under persistent snow cover encourages snow mold to develop. If you discover snow mold on your lawn in spring, rake it off. Disinfect the rake in a 10% bleach solution to prevent the spread of fungal spores.

Leaves that are "pancaked" onto grass during winter may suffocate the grass, resulting in bare spots in spring. So, in fall, rake leaves onto your garden beds as winter mulch or add them to the compost heap. Either way, they are as valuable to a gardener as gold.

Although many books propose fall lawn fertilizing, there are several reasons why this is not recommended for the prairies. If we have a mild fall, newly invigorated growth points risk being damaged when winter's cold temperatures eventually arrive. Like all hardy plants, grasses should go dormant in fall (yes, this means brown). Lush growth may also promote the development of snow mold. If the grass is dormant or the ground has frozen, then most of the fertilizer will just run off, doing the lawn no good and adding a pollution burden to waterways. Another caution against fall fertilizing is that trees or shrubs in or near the lawn may get a boost of growth at a time they too need to go dormant. Trees and shrubs are put at risk of excessive die-back if fertilizers are used in fall, particularly if the fertilizer has a high nitrogen content.

Winterizing Ponds

The process of winterizing a pond depends on whether the pond will be empty or kept full of water. Hardy lilies and fish can be successfully overwintered in the deep part of a pond if it doesn't freeze. Smaller ponds must either be emptied or heated with an agricultural stock-tank heater, pond heater, or a floating trough de-icer. Don't let water in small concrete ponds freeze solid—the ponds may crack! Mounting evidence suggests that, for in-ground, pre-formed plastic ponds and ponds constructed with flexible liners, leaving them filled with water protects them better than draining them and exposing them to winter conditions.

Prepare Pond Plants

Tender pond plants that will not survive a prairie winter should be brought inside or thrown on the compost heap.

If the pond is emptied, pull hardy potted plants out of the pond and bury the pots up to their rim elsewhere in the garden until spring. If the pond is kept full and heated or insulated against freezing, leave hardy water plants in place. Trim all dead foliage so that it does not fall in the pond and decompose.

TABLE 12: OVERWINTERING STRATEGIES FOR COMMON POND PLANTS

Common Name	Botanical Name	Overwintering Strategy
Duckweed	*Lemna minor*	Free floating, hardy; will sink to bottom of deep ponds; indoors, put in a lighted aquarium or stock pan with circulating water
Marsh marigold	*Caltha palustris*	Marginal plant; leave in ponds that will not freeze; otherwise, bury pot in garden for winter
Blue flag, yellow flag	*Iris versicolor, I. pseudacorus*	Marginal plant; leave in ponds that will not freeze; otherwise, bury pot in garden for winter
Pickerel weed	*Pontederia cordata*	Marginal plant, borderline hardiness; may survive in ponds that do not freeze
Umbrella palm	*Cyperus alternifolius*	Tropical; pull pot from pond before frost, winter indoors in a tub in a bright window
Water lily	*Nymphaea* spp.	Move hardy lilies to deep water where they will not freeze or store indoors in their pots, wrapped in damp newspaper in a fridge or other cool place (2 to 5°C, 35 to 41°F) until spring (check periodically to make sure they don't dry out). They can go back into the pond as soon as you can chip through the ice.

Protect Fish

If the pond is deep enough or heated, fish can remain outdoors all year; otherwise, they need different quarters. Outdoor fish are usually dormant below 5°C (41°F) and should not be fed.

If fish are wintered indoors, the minimum requirement is a large, unheated aquarium or other container suitable for the number and size of fish to be housed. It should be supplied with light, water circulation, and a cover to prevent the fish from jumping out. Your pond pump, if it is small enough, can supply the water circulation. If the fish are to be kept at room temperature, then suitable filtration is also needed. Ask you local aquarium store staff for assistance in selecting equipment and supplies.

Indoor fish need to be fed. Whether your fish are active or dormant, supply them with some hiding places using rocks, bricks, aquarium decor, or suitable aquatic plants. The fish will be less stressed and more likely to survive the winter in good condition.

Scoop Debris

Scoop out the accumulated debris. Decomposing debris robs the water of oxygen in spring and produces methane gas that is toxic to fish. Netting may be stretched over the top to keep leaves from blowing in during fall. This can be left on all winter or removed after all the leaves have fallen.

Drain Pond

Small concrete ponds that will not be heated should be emptied most of the way and lightly cleaned, but not scrubbed. Leave some water in the pond so that, in spring, you have some aged, debris-free water available to inoculate the pond with proper nutrients and bacteria. This will hasten the pond water's return to a natural balance.

Clean Pump

Remove and clean the pump. Then, store it, use it indoors for overwintering fish, or leave it running in your heated pond.

Make a Cover

For heated ponds, cut 5 cm (2 in.) thick Styrofoam™ to float on top of the water in the pond, but ensure there are open areas around the edge for gas exchange. This will give the fish some cover and help retain heat. It also gives winter birds a handy platform for accessing open water. An insulated cover over the whole pond may also prevent unheated ponds from freezing. Place boards over the pond and stack thick, insulating material, such as bales of hay, on top.

Heat Pond
Ponds can be heated using either a thermostatically controlled stock-tank or pond heater or a floating trough de-icer. Your local farm supply store will be a helpful source.

Defend Against Critters
Although the antics of squirrels and the lope of a white hare across a white lawn may delight some gardeners, others find the price of hosting furry (and hungry) critters too high. There are some ways to cope with the less charming side of visiting winter animals.

Voles and Mice
Voles and most mice are active all winter, creating a maze of tunnels in the warm layer where snow meets ground. Where snowfall is sparse, deep mulches offer protection for these rodents. It may be possible to tolerate a small number of them spending the winter under your rose huts, but few gardeners appreciate tender shrubs being used as winter food. Delay covering your tender shrubs until freeze-up has occurred to lessen the chances of them moving in. Keep feeder spillage swept up, or use feeders designed to keep spillage in and critters out.

Deer
Deer may nip branch tips. Usually, this natural pruning will not harm plants, although it may result in an oddly shaped shrub. Cedars are particularly tasty to deer and may be killed or completely disfigured by them. Wrap cedars loosely in burlap or, if you want to enjoy your cedars in winter, purchase products designed to render trees unpalatable. These products are available at garden centers. Many gardeners resort to home-made strategies to deter these animals, for example, hanging noisemakers or shiny objects (tin plates, old CDs) in trees. Some gardeners swear by hanging objects with a repellent scent, such as old pantyhose stuffed with human or pet hair. Deer will not jump over a fence if they cannot see what is on the other side. A 1.8-m (6-ft.) solid fence may keep them out.

Hares

In severe winters, or in years when hares are plentiful, small trees may have their bark chewed excessively by these animals. If their chewing completely girdles a tree, the tree may die. Wrap the tender trunks of young trees in tree wrap or chicken wire to the maximum height a hare can reach. Take snow depth into account when deciding how high to wrap the trunks.

Squirrels

Gardeners either hate them or love them. Some squirrels dig up and eat bulbs, and if you have feeders, squirrels will find and clean them out pretty quickly. Once the ground is frozen, your bulbs are protected. Until that time, cover planted areas with chicken wire or sprinkle these areas with blood meal, which squirrels avoid. Blood meal has to be reapplied periodically, at least until freeze-up. Depending on the animals present in your area, weigh the benefits of the cure against the ills—blood meal can attract omnivores and carnivores such as dogs, skunks, and raccoons.

Small ponds can be kept open all winter using a trough de-icer. A floating piece of Styrofoam™ retains some heat and provides thirsty birds with a landing pad.
NORA BRYAN

Consider feeding squirrels peanuts or sunflower seeds in their own feeder. They are more likely to leave bulbs and bird feeders alone if they have their own lunch counter. Otherwise, use squirrel-proof feeders or mount feeders on special poles that have squirrel baffles, although you may discover that some squirrels can defeat such elaborate schemes. Perhaps the acrobatics and antics of squirrels getting at a so-called squirrel-proof feeder are worth the price of a few seeds.

THE "SNOW EATER"

Warm, dry winds affect gardeners along the foothills of the Rocky Mountains from Calgary, Alberta, to Helena, Montana. These winds are called Chinooks, an aboriginal term meaning "snow eater," and they cause extreme temperature fluctuations. Although people welcome the warmth they bring, the rising temperatures are a sinister siren's call for woody plants. A long, warm Chinook occurring in early spring may cause buds to break dormancy, only to be killed when winter temperatures suddenly return. Flower buds are more susceptible than leaf buds. The best defense against Chinooks is to choose the hardiest cultivars available and to keep them healthy. Healthy plants will generate new growth, even if flower buds are lost for the year.

Seven

Avoiding Cabin Fever—
Things To Do Inside and Out

WINTER ON THE PRAIRIES LASTS MUCH LONGER than from the winter solstice (21 December) to the vernal equinox (21 March). Once you've caught up on last year's gardening magazines, cabin fever may set in and the pull of the garden may be too strong to resist. There are some winter gardening tasks to attend to—snow harvesting, dealing with ice build-up and heavy snowfalls, composting (both indoors and out)—but there are some fun projects, too, such as forcing winter bulbs indoors.

Making the Winter Garden Rounds

There is little to do in the winter garden once you've set up your winter scenes. Only a few outdoor tasks need pull you away from a comfy chair and a stack of gardening catalogues.

Snow Harvesting

Prairie gardeners are born with a snow shovel in their hands, but savvy gardeners shoveling the walkway after an overnight snowfall do not just fling snow willy-nilly. They engage in "snow harvesting," that is, moving snow around to cover exposed or dry sites, or to protect tender plants.

Pile this valuable winter mulch carefully on tender plants or stockpile it in a shady spot to use later. Since shoveled snow is heavier than snow that falls naturally, avoid piling too much on exposed shrubs, particularly junipers, to prevent branches from snapping. Shovel some snow under dry eaves to provide future moisture for plants close to the house and to prevent them from breaking dormancy too soon.

Plants are thrown into sharp relief,
enhancing their form under the low
angle of the winter sun.
BARBARA KAM

Traction Tricks

Sometimes ice builds up on our walkways no matter how diligently we shovel. What we use for traction on ice has gardening considerations. Salt is a general no-no if there is any risk of salty water draining into garden beds. Sand is a better choice. Choose sand that is made of pure quartz rather than sand that contains lime. The latter is usually dusty and fizzes in acid (e.g., vinegar or muriatic acid). Horticultural sand and most play sands are quartz rich. Avoid sand used to make cement. Another option is kitty litter, but not the clumping type. It contains bentonite clay, which is used to line ponds and is obviously not good for drainage. Don't sweep kitty litter into your garden beds—most prairie gardens contain enough clay. Other options for providing traction include wood shavings or vermiculite.

The de-icing salt that is used on public sidewalks or roadways will injure most plants if it is allowed to accumulate. Salt damage is often easy to diagnose because symptoms manifest themselves more strongly on the "salted" side of the plant. On deciduous plants, salt can kill growing tips and result in both stunted growth and the creation of many branches that are often referred to as "witch's brooms" due to their shape. On evergreens, last year's growth will appear purplish or brown if sprayed with salt. Salt damage on lawns is usually seen as browning where grass meets pavement.

To reduce salt damage in areas with well-drained soils, a good spring soaking may be able to flush the salts out of the root zone. However, this solution may be ineffective for other soil profiles. If you

A Tolleson's weeping juniper stands guard over some tender shrubs hidden under rose huts.
NORA BRYAN

have a thin layer of well-drained soil atop heavy clay subsoil, water can pool on top of the subsoil, collecting salt that has accumulated in the clay and actually "recharging" the topsoil with salt. If you have an area where salt exposure can't be avoided, choose salt-tolerant plants (see Table 13).

TABLE 13: SALT-TOLERANT PLANTS

Common Name	Botanical Name
Sea thrift	*Armeria* spp.
Black chokeberry	*Aronia melanocarpa*
Silver mound artemisia	*Artemisia schmidtiana*
Feather reed grass	*Calamagrostis* x *acutiflora*
Caragana	*Caragana* spp.
Russian olive	*Elaeagnus angustifolia*
Sea holly	*Eryngium* spp.
Blue fescue	*Festuca glauca*
Siberian salt tree	*Halimodendron halodendron*
Sea buckthorn	*Hippophae rhamnoides*
Juniper	*Juniperus* spp.
Sea lavender	*Limonium latifolium*
Colorado spruce	*Picea pungens* spp. and cultivars
Autumn Joy sedum	*Sedum* x 'Autumn Joy'
Silver buffaloberry	*Shepherdia argentea*

Dealing with Heavy Snowfalls and Ice

Although prairie snows are usually dry and light, if you didn't bind your columnar shrubs with netting, raffia, or (gasp) burlap, an occasional heavy snowfall can pull branches down and may break them. If a heavy, wet snowfall bends tree branches unduly, carefully brush the snow off. Woody ornamentals, like willow, birch, poplar, maple, and elm, and improperly pruned trees with water sprouts (suckers and witch's brooms) are susceptible to snow damage. Conifers are less at risk.

Ice coatings can increase branch weight by up to forty times. Don't whack ice off frozen trees; harsh action with the broom can snap frozen branches. Instead, prop up severely iced branches and tidy broken branches with a clean pruning cut. For minor damage, pruning can wait till just before spring. For birch and maple, given that sap will run out of wounds, the decision to prune now or after leaf-out is based on whether pruning will reduce or increase the number of open wounds.

Serious damage, including split trunks or large torn branches, may require an arborist's services for safety and tree health. Split trunks may need bracing. Some studies indicate that applying a complete fertilizer in very early spring during root growth will help speed recovery. Depending on the severity of the wounds, tree removal may be the best option. You then have the remainder of the winter to plan for a suitable replacement.

Checking Out the Winter Garden

For a true gardening enthusiast, an occasional tramp through the winter garden can be like a snack tiding you over till the sumptuous fare of the growing season arrives. On warmer days, it may take just a few minutes to go outside and pull the seed heads that gave a few months of extended pleasure but now appear bent and beaten by the driven snow. These can be added to the compost heap or, if your compost never cooks enough to kill seeds, put into the bird feeder.

Alternating freeze-thaw cycles can disturb the soil and heave some plants right out of the ground. If you discover exposed plants and the ground is too solid to work, cover them well with whatever is available (snow, leaves, carpeting) until the ground thaws and then replant them.

On sunny days, stroll around the neighborhood. For inspiration, look at what your neighbors have done in their winter gardens. Visit your local botanical garden for even more winter ideas.

Composting in Winter

Although it's hard to think about compost when the contents of your bin are a solid block, much of the compostable waste we create in our kitchens during the dark season does not have to go to a landfill. Here are two options for winter composting.

Vermicomposting

Vermicomposting is a fancy name for having worms eat your garbage. Indoor composting is ideal for northern gardeners who do not wish to trudge out to their compost bins in winter. Done properly, the process is odorless and results in wonderful compost.

Composting worms are red wigglers (*Eisenia foetida* or *Lumbricus rubellus*), which reproduce quickly and consume their weight daily. Check fishing supply shops and recycling stores for stock.

Worms are kept in a bin filled with bedding material. Bedding options include shredded cardboard, newsprint, and peat. Soak the material in water until it is soggy; at that point, squeeze out the water until only a few drops seep between your fingers. Put one or two handfuls of soil or finely ground eggshells on the bottom of the bin as grit to aid the worms' digestion and place the bedding on top. Wait 24 hours, and then distribute the worms on top of the bedding. Check the bin periodically and add moisture if the bedding is drying out.

Bins can be kept in the kitchen, a closet, the basement, or a heated garage. You can purchase a kit or use a wooden or plastic container that is 20 to 30 cm (8 to 12 in.) deep and has a lid. Drill air holes in the lid. (Don't worry; worms hate light so they won't crawl out.)

Feed the worms about 500 mL (2 cups) of food waste once or twice a week. Let your nose be your guide: if it starts to smell, you may have added more food than the system can handle. Add the same scraps you would add to an outdoor composter: peelings, eggshells, tea bags, lint, etc., but not animal products. Avoid tropical fruit peels that seem to spontaneously generate fruit flies. Bury the waste under 5 cm (2 in.) of bedding. The next time you feed them, bury the food beside the previous spot so the worms do not have far to travel. By the time you rotate through the bin, your first deposit of food scraps will be mostly gone.

To harvest the compost, push the ready compost to one side of the bin and fill the other side with fresh bedding. Add food only to the new area. In a couple of months, most of your worms will have relocated so you can remove the compost and add fresh bedding. You can also "divide and dump" by removing two-thirds of the compost and retaining one-third for worm regeneration.

Regular Composting

Regular composting can continue throughout the winter. Dump your scraps in the compost bin as usual, remembering to layer your greens (fruit and vegetable peelings, vacuum bag contents, tea and coffee grounds) and browns (dried leaves, sawdust, hair, and feathers). Browns can be saved from your fall cleanup in bags until you need to apply a layer (or chunk, depending on the temperature). Everything freezes in place and will thaw in the appropriate mixture come spring.

Alternatively, save your browns and greens in large buckets for spring mixing. Plastic lids can crack in the cold, making the contents vulnerable to neighborhood critters, so keep lids in place with rocks or bricks. By spring, you may have slurry to add to your bin. Although it may smell initially, consider it a jumpstart in the decomposition process. The proper mixing of two to three volumes of browns (such as leaves) with one volume of greens (such as kitchen scraps) should reduce the odor quickly.

WINTER "TO-DO" LIST

- Visit web sites, peruse catalogues, stare out your window, and imagine. Notice bare spots in your garden. Organize and review notes from earlier seasons.
- Continue adding material to your compost pile or feed your worms.
- Save your Christmas tree and "plant" it in a drift for winter interest and shelter for birds, or use its branches as mulch or to bulk up your winter containers.
- Read the gardening books and magazines you set aside during the growing season.
- "Harvest" snow for garden beds and to use against south-facing walls; bring some indoors and melt it to water your houseplants.
- Walk about your neighborhood and visit botanical gardens on warmer days to note interesting winter plant combinations.
- Prune woody ornamentals after dormancy (in late winter or early spring), excluding birches, maples, and shrubs that flower on last year's growth.
- Make a winter container or a wreath (see Chapter Eight).
- Check for frost heaving during warm spells. Put heaved plants back into the ground, if possible, and apply a thick mulch after the soil re-freezes.
- Check bulbs, corms, and pond plants that are being overwintered indoors. Add moisture if required or replace the storage medium if it is too wet.
- Make occasional rounds outdoors to see if snow or ice build-up needs to be cleared from branches or gutters.
- If you have a running pond, make sure circulation and heaters are working properly.
- Keep bird feeders topped and provide birds with an open source of water for drinking. Consider using a birdbath heater.
- Bring the outside in by forcing bulbs or taking cuttings of forsythia, lilac, or other branches.
- Start seeds indoors.

Bringing the Outdoors In

During late winter, when spring seems eternally just around the corner, forcing branches or bulbs into bloom indoors in a vase may take the edge off a northern gardener's impatience. Two projects are included here.

Forcing Forsythia (and other flowering shrubs and trees)

Generally, plants can be coaxed into blooming about one to two months ahead of their natural schedule—between February and April for the northernmost prairies. This is referred to as "forcing." Forsythia branches harvested close to their natural bloom schedule are easier to coax than those taken earlier in winter. The process can take from one to eight weeks. Branches from fruit trees, flowering almonds and plums, pussy willows, lilacs, and mock oranges are also amenable to the process—just keep in mind their natural bloom schedule.

Begin the process by checking to see if the buds have started swelling on your shrub. If they have, select branches that are 25 cm (10 in.) or longer and cut them back to the joining stem, being careful not to ruin the shrub's overall appearance.

To avoid rot, remove any side branches that will be below the water line in the vase you have chosen to use. Re-cut the end of each branch at a slant or smash it with a hammer. Place the branches in the vase in very cold water to avoid shock if daytime temperatures have yet to rise above freezing.

Put your arrangement in an area with indirect light and cool nighttime temperatures. Replace the water in the vase every few days, using tepid water. Re-cut the ends of the branches weekly to encourage water uptake.

Forcing Paperwhites in Water

Paperwhites (sold as *Narcissus tazetta* or *N. papyraceus*) are some of the easiest bulbs to force since they do not require a chilling period. These flowers are tall and strongly scented, and people either like or dislike their perfume.

Select firm, healthy bulbs for planting in groups. Store them in a cool, dark place between 3 and 10°C (35 and 50°F). If you are not planning to use them immediately, keep them away from ripening fruit, as it gives off ethylene gas that can hinder bulb flowering.

Containers should be wide in proportion to the plant's expected height to reduce the risk of tipping. As the paperwhites grow, it may be necessary to tie them together with ribbon or raffia to keep them upright. Another elegant option is to use a clear glass vase taller than the cultivar being forced. The sides create a stylish support for the tall stems and heavy leaves while providing a window on the blooms and roots. In any case, do not use a container with drainage holes.

Use rinsed gravel, marbles, polished rock, or glass to anchor the bulb roots in the container bottom. Place the bulbs on the medium, pointy-side up and as close together as possible without touching. Cover the bulbs with the remaining medium, leaving only their very tips exposed. Add water to just below the base of the bulb to avoid rot. Fertilizer is not necessary, as the bulb provides its own nutrients for blooming.

Place the potted bulbs in a cool, bright room, or put them in a dark room for the first week to encourage stronger root development to anchor these tall plants. Periodically top up the water. Rotate the container by 45 degrees weekly so the bulbs do not lean toward the light and tip. Dispose of the bulbs when the blooms are spent.

Plant new containers periodically to have blooms throughout winter. Paperwhites take approximately five or six weeks to bloom. Use your calendar and work backward to have blooms for special occasions. Ultra-organized people mark the containers with the bulb type and planting date.

O CHRISTMAS TREE!

Many people celebrate Christmas with a real tree. But when the tree comes down, it does not have to go directly to the dump or to your area's recycling program. A "used" Christmas tree still has value.

TEMPORARY TREE If you have a large deck or a naked view, either place the tree in an empty pot on your deck or stand it in a snow bank in your sight line. Voilà! Instant green. If the tree is too big for the empty spot, simply chop it down to scale.

ADDITIONAL GREENERY Boughs added to a winter arrangement make it appear lush and green. Depending on the size of your container, you can make a simple winter arrangement just by filling it full of boughs.

WINTER MULCH De-limb old Christmas trees and pile the boughs onto small shrub roses and any other plants that need extra winter protection. The boughs are perfect for windswept areas where supposedly "evergreen" groundcovers desiccate as their snow cover blows away.

PLANT SUPPORTS Lay boughs atop tender fern heads. Come spring, the needles slowly drop and the floppy fronds grow up between the branches.

GROUNDCOVERS If you are a keen gardener, let the tree dry out and, using a heavily gloved hand, knock off its needles near the start of spring. The needles provide an attractive and natural summer mulch that is perfect for woodland gardens. You may not want to do this if your tree has been sprayed with fire retardants or green coloring, however. Ask about this when you buy your tree.

The red and green theme of this container of conifer boughs, curly willow, real and artificial berries, and seasonal ornamentation is a classic combination for winter.
BARBARA KAM

Evergreen conifers purchased at end-of-season prices replace summer's annuals.
BARBARA KAM

Baskets, emptied of summer annuals, do double duty stuffed with boughs and berries.
BARBARA KAM

Eight

Winter Arrangements—
Containers and Wreaths

WINTER ARRANGEMENTS ARE WONDERFUL additions to the winterscape. They add color and texture to what might otherwise be a barren landscape and bring pleasure to the viewer whether from inside or outside the house. This chapter includes instructions for creating a simple but classic container arrangement and for putting together a wreath to hang in your winter garden, as well as tips on how to gather material throughout the year to add to your winter arrangements.

Winter Containers

Container gardening has grown in popularity over the past several years because of its adaptability. Containers work on large estates and tiny balconies, depending on their scale. In spring, there is a great frenzy to create beautiful containers with annuals that can then be moved easily to areas of the garden that require a splash of color when perennial blooms fade. This same principle of adaptability applies when creating winter containers. With some foresight and a bit of effort, you can create winter containers and other greenery, such as wreaths, garlands, or swags, that will not only enhance the view from your window but also your home's curb appeal. In fact, containers play a stronger role in the winter garden than in the summer garden, as arrangements are more dramatic against the monochromatic backdrop of a dull winter's day.

Rather than trying to figure out how to help plants cheat death, accept the inevitable and use non-living plant materials for your winter containers. These containers are like low-maintenance flower arrangements; there is no need to water, fertilize, or deadhead. All the effort is in the setup. It's a fun project and relatively quick to do. And, although you may be tempted to move your silk plants outdoors, pink fuchsia hanging baskets look artificial in the depths of winter, no matter how realistic the arrangement may seem in summer. Other more seasonally appropriate options exist. Many of the materials may be available in your own yard.

Just as in summer, you can put containers where you want them. For instance, move them from against the house where they sat during the growing season to where they can be admired from the kitchen or great room window. There is no point putting effort into something that will not be visible. Winter containers at the front door greet guests with welcoming color, while large planters on either side of the garage add dramatic curb appeal.

Let's not forget hanging baskets. Inexpensive plastic containers or baskets lined with moss or a coco (coir) product can also be used during the winter season. Stuff greenery and ornaments in the top for a traditional look or fill the top and cover the sides and bottom, as well, for a ball of greenery.

Finally, extra containers make good garden ornaments on their own. Tip them over and stack them in interesting ways.

A WORD ABOUT POTS

Most containers will survive freeze-thaw cycles for several years with some help. Porous containers absorb water during the summer, and if they freeze later, they may expand and break. To reduce the risk, allow these containers to dry out at the end of the growing season. Some lightly fired pottery pieces may not withstand harsh winters; either store them or treat them as short-term investments needing periodic replacement. You decide if the added beauty to the garden over the years is adequate return for the cost of the pot.

Both Italian and Mexican terracotta pots may continue to survive outdoors for more than ten and five years, respectively. Wicker and plastic containers can be used year-round for several years before cracking or disintegrating. Metal and wood might survive indefinitely.

A Classic Winter Arrangement

Although there is no limit to the style of winter container arrangements you could devise, here is a simple but effective recipe to get you started.

Prepare the Container First, remove the dead annuals from the container. Then, either loosen the soil, ensuring it is dry, or completely empty the container. You can use soil, sand, or something similar to anchor your arrangement or you can work with an empty container. If you decide to work with an empty container, you will need longer branches and more of them to keep the arrangement standing (the branches will "knit" together). Before you start creating your arrangement, put the planter where it will be seen to best advantage, either from inside your house or from the curb.

Gather Plants and Supplies Collect a generous amount of evergreen boughs, a number of long branches, such as bright red or yellow dogwood twigs, and an assortment of stems with seed heads and berries. Chances are you will need more than you originally estimated. You can add bows, seasonal ornaments, and even small twinkle lights. Wear gloves for protection from sharp needles and thorns. Keep a pair of light pruners handy for shortening branches or trimming excess. Wire or floral tape is helpful for adding ornaments.

Create the Basic Form The most effective arrangements—summer or winter—create a triangle or pyramid in the pot. This means tall plants in the center (or back), surrounded by greenery of medium height, and then by edging plants to widen and soften the edge of the container. The arrangement should be in scale with the size of the pot.

Evergreen boughs are the equivalent of summer lobelia or geraniums that provide greenery and fullness while softening the edges of the planter. Place the greenery thickly around the pot's circumference. Next come the long twigs of dogwood or a similar shrub; these are like the spike of summer dracaena, adding height to the arrangement. Place them in the center of the pot if you will be viewing it from several sides or at the back if it is set against a wall. For scale and proportion, the twigs should be two to three times the height of the pot, and the evergreens should extend to about one and a half to two times the width of the pot from tip to tip.

Depending on whether you are using a tall, narrow pot or a low, squat one, the proportions of your display can be tall and narrow, wide and full, or even asymmetrical.

Add Details Complete your arrangement with the various seed heads and berries you have gathered. The trick is to clump your "flowers," which is a bonus if you lack floral arranging skills. Clumping entails simply grabbing a group of the same seed heads and stuffing them in a single spot; it is much easier to appreciate their color and texture this way. For example, individual twigs of rose hips interspersed throughout the arrangement on your front step will not make much of an impression on houseguests being quickly ushered in from the cold. The red of the rose hips will be far more obvious if you clump them; you will have a much more effective arrangement.

Show Your Style Depending on your taste, you can further decorate your containers. String twinkle lights through the branches to draw attention to them. Use lights shaped like pumpkin lanterns for Halloween, gourds for Thanksgiving, and hearts for Valentine's Day to honor different themes. For a natural look, include artificial berries and birds; for more glamour, include glitter-, gold-, or silver-sprayed branches in your arrangement. Add ornaments, ribbons, and bows. You can choose beyond the traditional Christmas plaids for color tones that match your front door or house trim. Your imagination is your only limit.

If you are working with wire hanging baskets, insert greens and berries into the sides and bottom of the liner. After you're done, water your arrangements so that the branches freeze in place and do not slip out due to gravity. It can take some practice to get a planter looking thick around the bottom. Raffia and ribbon tucked into the bare spaces can fill out the look. You can also attach berries and cones with florist's wire.

If this all sounds like too much work, simply purchase potted evergreens at the end of the growing season and place them in your most weatherproof planters. Since they are live plants, you may want to water them so they can prepare for freeze-up and then water them again if the container should thaw. (This can happen a few times throughout the winter if the sun warms the sides of the pot.) These evergreens may overwinter successfully, but it is best to treat them as annuals. That way, you will be pleasantly surprised should they survive into spring, instead of being disappointed when they start turning brown.

CREATING WINTER CONTAINERS—A SUMMARY

- Remove dead annuals.
- Loosen soil, ensuring it is dry.
- Move pot(s) to their winter location.
- Place evergreens around the perimeter.
- Place tall twigs in the center or back.
- Add seed heads, berries, and ornaments.
- Clump; don't fuss.

Wreaths

Although wreaths have a strong association with Advent and Christmas, the symbology of the wreath, or circle, predates these holidays. In fact, the wreath and circle are nearly universal cultural and religious symbols, representing eternity, victory, committed love, and the circle of life. The meaning of a wreath can also depend on its materials. The olive wreath, part of the United Nations logo, is a symbol of victory and peace. Winners of ancient Greek Olympics received such a wreath, and wars stopped during these games to allow athletes of all nations to compete. A wreath of laurel signifies distinction in the arts or military, while ivy denotes geniality. A wreath or swag made of wheat honors the harvest and the promise of next year's season. Today, many people hang a wreath on their door or in their house as a year-round sign of welcome.

In winter, many prairie householders hang evergreen wreaths on their doors at Christmas, then remove them after the holiday season. But these items can add seasonal décor for the entire winter. In fact, look beyond doors for other places to display them. If you clean up annual vines and late-blooming clematis in fall, you may find yourself with a suddenly bare fence. A wreath, swag, or garland can add visual interest to it. Add berries, seeds, and grains to the arrangements and you can attract birds. Garlands also look great draped over balcony railings.

You can buy undecorated wreaths, swags, and garlands from florists and garden centers and add your personal touch to them, or you can make a wreath from scratch.

Winter Wreath Project

Gather Basic Materials You will need several evergreen boughs, cut in varying lengths, from about 15 to 20 cm (6 to 8 in.); a base, such as a florist's foam or wire form or a grapevine wreath; and something to connect the materials to the base, such as thread, fishing line, or thin wire (available from craft and hardware stores). Use gloves since some boughs are prickly.

Lay on the Background Take three to five evergreen boughs and tie their stems together. Lay this bundle on your base and fan the boughs until they cover it. When you're satisfied with their placement, secure the bundle to the wreath with thread. Ideally, you can do this with a single knot on the first clump and then just twine and spiral the thread securely for each additional bundle. Continue grouping boughs and layering them on your base, going in the same direction as the original bunch. How closely you layer your boughs depends on their length and density and your personal taste. As you lay the boughs, hide the thread under various stems. Once you've completed the circle and are back at the starting point, you may have to fuss with the boughs a bit to make them flow nicely. Give them a good final wrap with the thread and tie several knots.

If the wreath is not secure enough for your liking, knot the thread or twist the wire at various intervals. However, if you can get away without extra knotting, spring cleanup is a cinch. Simply hold the wreath in a garbage bag and give the thread or fishing line a few snips; this causes the whole thing to unravel and fall into the bag. Your form is now ready for the following winter.

Determine the Top Look critically at your wreath to decide which is the top and which is the bottom. At your designated top, twine thread or wire around the base, still hiding it under the boughs. Make a loop to use for hanging the wreath, either at the top or the back of the base. If you used light thread for tying, you may want something heavier to support the weight of the wreath.

Spice It Up If your wreath has the odd sparse patch, you can go back and insert more boughs. Alternatively, these are perfect spots to add berries, rose hips, dried flower sprays, such as lady's mantle, statice, or baby's breath, nuts, pinecones, bows, and other ornaments.

CREATING WREATHS—A SUMMARY

- Collect the basic materials.
- Fan the boughs across the base of the wreath and fasten them.
- Continue layering evergreens till the base is covered.
- Find the top and add a loop to hang your wreath.
- Add seed heads, berries, and ornaments.

Gathering Materials Year-round

Whether you are designing a winter container or a wreath, the collection procedures for materials are the same. During your summer rounds of dead-heading (removing spent flowers), save the flower heads that are attractive. For example, consider saving those of lady's mantle, teasel, some echinacea, and some poppies. If you find that some of your plants with attractive flowers or seed heads disintegrate or fade rather quickly, you may want to take a few cuttings of these in summer. The flowers of sea holly, globe thistle, and Russian sage maintain their blue tones longer if they are cut when fresh. Tie them with string and hang them upside down in your garden shed or garage. Prune snippets of baby's breath, statice, and hydrangea and save them for your winter arrangements. Store them in a paper bag in a cool, dry place. Don't forget to collect the interesting seed heads of plants that are outside your winter sight lines.

It is safe to prune most trees and shrubs once they are dormant. For example, pruning out the oldest 20% of dogwood twigs per year is often recommended because young twigs have the brightest color; essentially, this creates a new shrub every five years. You can use these pruned branches for your winter containers. Save the cuttings from evergreens that creep onto your sidewalk or driveway when you tidy their shape. When trimming your junipers, angle the cut in toward the branch—missing the needles—for a natural look. Avoid removing entire branches from the bottom of a spruce. They will not grow back and you will be left with a view of bare ground beneath the tree. While you are at it, offer to tidy up evergreens and shrubs for agreeable neighbors. If you still do not have enough evergreens and branches, there are several other options. You can purchase boughs from a florist, contact an arborist about picking up prunings, check alleys for prunings in fall, or wait until after December and recycle a Christmas tree.

CONTAINER AND WREATH TIPS

DESICCATION DOS If cedars and other evergreens desiccate in the sun and wind in your area, cuttings in containers and wreaths will be affected similarly. To reduce the effects, don't use cedar cuttings in containers that are in the sun and wind, mist your arrangements occasionally, and try an anti-desiccant spray. The sprays are often available where Christmas trees are sold.

SNOW WHAT If your area gets lots of wet, heavy snow, stick with sturdy evergreens, branches, and ornaments that can withstand the weight of new snow in open areas. You can use lighter, more delicate material for arrangements that will be sheltered by eaves or tree branches.

DEER DEFENSE If deer eat your arrangements in summer, you may have similar issues in winter. Just as there are no such things as "deer-proof" containers in summer, the same applies to winter designs. However, by anchoring the plants in soil, the twigs may freeze in, making it more difficult for the deer to pull the entire arrangement out.

ITEMS FOR WINTER ARRANGEMENTS

From the Garden
- allium seed heads
- Amur cherry stems and fruit
- cotoneaster stems and berries
- crabapple stems and fruit
- cattail seed heads (spray with hairspray or gloss first)
- echinacea or echinops seed heads
- everlastings
- statice, both perennial and annual
- hops' seed heads
- juniper, pine, cedar, or other evergreen prunings*
- liatris seed heads
- mountain ash stems and berries
- red-* or yellow-twigged dogwood stems
- rose hips*
- sea buckthorn berries
- silver buffaloberry (white twigs on male, berries on female)
- lady's mantle seed heads
- poppy seed heads
- willow stems

From the Florist
- curly willow
- eucalyptus, green or red
- pepperberry
  (Note: holly berries are not recommended as they blacken after killing frosts)

Miscellaneous
- dried gourds or fruits*
- feathers
- pine cones*
- seasonal ornaments
- twinkle lights
- wire ribbon*
- strung cranberries
*Also available from florists

Blue spruce and yellow willow twigs are used to create this window box's blue and gold theme. Spruce cones, mountain ash berries, and a few seasonal ribbons add flourish.
NORA BRYAN

EVERLASTINGS

Everlastings are aptly named because the flowers keep their color and form very well even when dried; they seemingly never die. Many have a straw or paperlike texture to their flowers. Everlastings can be either perennial or annual, although we usually think of annuals. Some can be sown outdoors, while others must be purchased in order to create an effective summer or winter display. Many people grow or buy everlasting flowers for crafts, and they are perfect additions to winter arrangements.

Add a few everlastings to mixed borders, containers, or your cutting garden. In the winter, the sturdier ones can be left standing, while others are best added to containers and protected from heavy snows. To dry everlastings, cut them before they are fully open, remove some of the lower leaves, hang them upside down to dry in small bunches, in a dry, dark place. We list several perennial everlastings in the plant portraits.

TABLE 14: ANNUAL EVERLASTINGS WORTH TRYING

Botanical name	Common Name
Ammobium alatum	winged everlasting
Helichrysum bracteatum	strawflower
Briza maxima, B. minor	large and lesser quaking grass
Celosia argentea	cockscomb
Coix lacryma-jobi	Job's tears
Gomphrena globosa	globe amaranth
Lagurus ovatus	bunny tail grass
Limonium sinuatum	annual statice
Lunaria annua (syn. *L. biennis*)	silver dollar, honesty, money plant (seed heads)
Melinis repens (syn. *Rhynchelytrum roseum*)	ruby grass
Moluccella laevis	bells of Ireland
Nigella damascena	love-in-a-mist (seed heads)
Papavar spp.	poppy (seed heads)
Pennisetum setaceum	fountain grass
Psylliostachys suworowii	Russian statice
Rhodanthe chlorocephala subsp. *rosea* (syn. *Helipterum roseum*)	rose everlasting
Xeranthemum annuum	common immortelle

Nine

Hosting Winter Visitors

WINTER TEARS THE LAST WITHERED LEAVES FROM OUR TREES, exposing their bare forms. All seems quiet except for a few small hearty birds picking their way up and down the bare branches. Looking up, a flock of birds may be discovered flitting and chattering away, picking at frozen mountain ash berries. A trail of animal prints cuts across the snowy yard. In our bleakest season, there is life after all.

Winter Visitors

Some birds, such as redpolls, visit only in winter, migrating back to the far north in summer. Other birds, such as grosbeaks, may visit urban feeders in winter but return to nearby natural areas in summer to breed, when their natural food sources become abundant once again.

Even though there are few wild mammals that visit urban gardens, gardeners may delight (or not) in the visits of a few furry characters. Rural and suburban gardeners might discover larger animals like deer, coyotes, and foxes in their gardens. And while some interactions with visiting animals might be delightful, others are not. Rural gardeners may have plenty of natural shrubbery to share with hungry animals—urban and suburban gardeners usually don't, preferring not to share their most prized shrubs and trees with hungry deer (see p. 64).

Color, movement, and the cheery sound of birds in the dead of winter can be yours for the price of a few sprinkled seeds. Well, that is a slight exaggeration. As with any gardening endeavor, a bit of thought and planning will produce a more pleasing result. Think like an animal. Animals need food, water, a place to wash up, cover from the elements, and protection from predators—exactly what you yourself would need if you were skulking around in people's back yards. You might not choose to meet all their needs, but the more elements you do provide, the greater the diversity of creatures you will attract.

Winter feeding need not be confined to birds. However, deliberately feeding predators such as coyotes is not recommended as it encourages them to lose their fear of man.

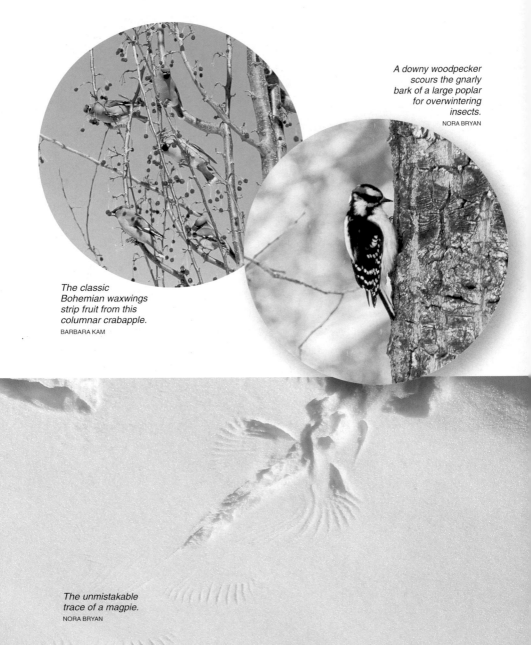

A downy woodpecker scours the gnarly bark of a large poplar for overwintering insects.
NORA BRYAN

The classic Bohemian waxwings strip fruit from this columnar crabapple.
BARBARA KAM

The unmistakable trace of a magpie.
NORA BRYAN

TABLE 15: BIRDS IN A WINTER GARDEN

The following table lists the birds most likely to be found in a prairie winter garden. If your garden is near the mountains or near large bodies of water, you may have other birds visit, including overwintering ducks or geese. Sometimes birds that normally migrate, such as robins, will also overwinter. In early spring, migrating birds may be seen in yards as they stop by to feed where food is available.

Bird	Season	Garden Notes
Gray partridge (*Perdix perdix*)	All year	May be seen in gardens with good cover near natural areas
Downy woodpecker (*Picoides pubescens*)	All year	Attracted to suet feeders
Hairy woodpecker (*Picoides villosus*)	All year	Similar to downy woodpecker, seen less commonly
Northern flicker (*Colaptes auratus*)	Some overwinter	Enjoys suet feeders, often feeds from ground during thaws
Blue jay (*Cyanocitta cristata*)	All year	Enjoys peanuts
Black-billed magpie (*Pica pica*)	All year	Omnivorous, attracted to suet feeders, peanuts, pet food
Common raven (*Corvus corax*)	All year	Wary bird, may venture into cities in winter, omnivorous
Black-capped chickadee (*Poecile atricapillus*)	All year	Enjoys sunflower seeds and shelled broken peanuts
Red-breasted nuthatch (*Sitta canadensis*)	Many overwinter	At home amongst conifers, enjoys sunflower seeds, broken peanuts
White-breasted nuthatch (*Sitta carolinensis*)	All year	Similar to above, more at home in deciduous trees
European starling (*Sturnus vulgaris*)	All year	Non-native bird, omnivorous, may displace native birds
Bohemian waxwing (*Bombycilla garrulus*)	Winter	Large flocks visit intermittently for a day or two, stripping crabapples and mountain ash berries
Pine grosbeak (*Pinicola enucleator*)	Winter	May visit gardens in harsh winters, enjoys seeds and berries
Common redpoll (*Carduelis flammea*)	Winter	Large flocks attracted to thistle tube feeders, not seen every year
Pine siskin (*Carduelis pinus*)	All year or winter only	Sometimes in the company of redpolls
Evening grosbeak (*Coccothraustes vespertinus*)	Winter	May feed from unroofed feeders, also eats berries and conifer seeds
House (English) sparrow (*Passer domesticus*)	All year	Non-native bird attracted to any type of feeder food; aggressive towards smaller birds

Feeders and Food

Long gone are the days of merely tossing out bread scraps to feed our feathered friends. This simply will not do. Now, birds are accustomed to better fare, and both feeder and seed choice can be bewildering. An analytical eye cast over store shelves reveals that seed feeders usually fall into one of four categories: tray feeders (with or without roofs), hopper-style feeders, tube feeders, and satellite feeders. Which is best? It depends on the types of birds you want to feed. There are advantages to each, and the birds have their own preferences, as shown in Table 16.

TABLE 16: BIRD FEEDER STYLES

Feeder Style	Description	Attracts	Pros and Cons
Tray	A flat surface, with or without a roof	Most birds; uncovered tray feeders situated low to the ground may attract ground feeders such as juncos and partridges	Pros: easy to make; readily used by most birds Cons: seed eaten quickly; uncovered seed may spoil or be covered in snow; seed must be put out each day
Hopper style	A central reservoir holds seed, which is released through small openings at the bottom into a tray. A roof protects the reservoir and tray. Variations include octagonal or round "gazebo-style" feeders	All small, perching birds such as chickadees and sparrows	Pros: does not need filling often; seed protected from weather Cons: aggressive birds like house sparrows may monopolize feeder
Tube (and thistle tube)	A clear plastic tube with feeding holes and perches; ones with tiny holes used for thistle seed	Chickadees, nuthatches, grosbeaks, and finches	Pros and Cons: same as hopper-style feeder; thistle tube used for thistle (niger) excludes sparrows
Satellite	A small, spherical plastic feeder with seed ports on its underside	Chickadees and nuthatches	Pros: designed to prevent aggressive birds like house sparrows from using it Cons: only contains a small amount of seed
Peanut cage	An open wire cage that holds shelled peanuts	Chickadees, nuthatches, downy and hairy woodpeckers	Pros: if properly mounted will discourage squirrels and sparrows Cons: peanuts may spoil if left out too long

TABLE 17: BIRD FOOD

Food	Attracts
Black oil and striped sunflower seeds	Chickadees, nuthatches, and house sparrows
Thistle, niger, or nyger	Redpolls and pine siskins
Wild bird food mixes (usually a mixture of millet, cracked corn, sunflower, and milo seeds)	House sparrows; others if preferred foods are not available
White and red millet	Gray-crowned rosy finches, redpolls, partridges, starlings, and house sparrows
Red milo	House sparrows
Peanut pieces	Chickadees, nuthatches, woodpeckers, and blue jays
Whole peanuts	Magpies, crows, ravens, and blue jays
Cracked corn	Partridges and blue jays
Suet and meat scraps	Woodpeckers, nuthatches, chickadees, blue jays, magpies, and ravens

Once you have selected your feeders, you need to stock them with suitable seeds. Sunflower seeds are, hands down, the best seeds to offer your birds. There are two types: the smaller black oil seed and the more familiar striped seed. Although it is often suggested that birds prefer the smaller oil seed type because it is easier to crack, some feeder operators and their avian guests disagree. Offering both types of seed solves the dilemma and allows the birds to choose.

Niger or nyger (niger is Latin for "black") is a small, black tropical seed that is sold as thistle. It is the favorite feeder food for small finches such as redpolls and siskins. A tube thistle feeder is the best type for serving this delicacy since its openings are too small for any other kind of seed.

Red and white millets are the small, round seeds commonly available in mixed "wild bird" food. Although not favored by most birds, they will eat them, if halfheartedly. The exceptions are ground-feeding birds, such as juncos and house sparrows, which seem to enjoy them. Red milo, the larger, reddish seed found in generalized wild-bird mixes, is even less favored by prairie birds except for—you guessed it—house sparrows.

Suet is another popular choice for bird feeders. Suet is the dense fat around the internal organs of cattle and sheep, but any animal fat can be called suet. Many insect-eating birds relish suet in winter. Suet

A red-breasted nuthatch, in a typical upside-down pose, enjoys a peanut butter and cornmeal mixture from this homemade log feeder.
NORA BRYAN

The familiar and endearing chickadee delights in shelled peanuts.
NORA BRYAN

*A pine siskin (right)
shares thistle from
a tube feeder with
its close cousin, the
redpoll (left).*
NORA BRYAN

feeders can be as sturdy as specially designed metal cages or as simple as onion bags. There is a debate about whether commercial suet cakes are inferior to natural chunks of suet. Commercial suet cakes are composed of rendered suet, which means it has been liquefied and cooled. Seeds and nuts are commonly added. Rendered suet resists spoiling longer than fresh suet. If you want to try preparing your own avian cuisine, you can render your own suet and add delicacies, as you desire.

Dedicated birders will want to include a peanut feeder, an elongated tube or metal cage filled with peanut pieces. These are a favorite of nuthatches and chickadees, which cling to their side to peck out peanut morsels. Unsalted, blanched peanuts found in the bulk section of the grocery store are preferred over non-food-grade peanuts sold with bird food.

Some gardeners are not happy hosting just another Joe's Diner along the avian highway and provide a gourmet restaurant instead. Live or roasted mealworms, hot-water-plumped raisins, and various nutmeats might attract some highbrow visitors. When a snowstorm hits in spring, returning birds will appreciate the extra nutritional content of these special treats, and you'll feel good knowing that you've helped to give them an extra chance at survival.

Water

Open water in winter is an often overlooked "bird magnet." Birds will flock to open water the way tourists flock to hot tubs. If you have a pond, consider keeping it open all winter by using a trough de-icer or a stock-tank heater. These inexpensive heaters are readily available from farm supply stores. Keep your pump running if you can, since birds find running water even more attractive than standing water. Although it is not practical to keep a large fountain or stream running in winter, a small stream of water spouting from a "spitter" and splashing into a pond can be accomplished easily. A nicely contoured piece of Styrofoam™ floated on the surface of the pond will help keep heat in and provide a convenient platform for thirsty birds.

Birdbaths can be kept open all winter with a specially designed thermostatic heater. Homemade winter birdbaths can be constructed with materials found around the home, using light bulbs as a heat source. Consult some of the books listed at the back of this book for plans and ideas.

Cover

Birds are attracted to gardens that have trees and shrubs. This is the environment in which they feel most secure. Even ground-feeding birds like to have shrubs nearby to use as cover if the shadow of a hawk passes overhead. Athletic cats may consider bird feeders to be lunch counters, so place low feeders about 3 m (10 ft.) from any source of feline concealment. If your garden has a minimal amount of shrubbery, create a temporary brush pile out of prunings and old Christmas trees for winter birds to use.

Place your bird feeders out of the brunt of winter winds. Dense conifers, especially spruce, also provide birds with extremely important protection from cold winds. If you lack suitable conifers or other cover in your garden, construct small, roofed shelters with perches and place them where they will shelter birds from the prevailing winds.

Nature's Bounty

The most natural way to encourage birds to visit your yard is by planting an abundance of berry- and seed-producing trees and shrubs. Many birds also eagerly seek the seed heads of stout annuals and perennials. The enduring stalks and brown heads of many herbaceous plants provide small birds with an important variety of seeds in the face of winter severity. Birds such as downy woodpeckers, chickadees, and nuthatches meticulously scrutinize older, gnarled trees that have exfoliating or deeply creviced bark. Trees such as poplar, aspen, and willow are eagerly scoured for overwintering insects or insect eggs.

INTRUDER ALERT!

Although any bird pecking at our feeders in the coldest days of winter is a delight, the house sparrow (*Passer domesticus*) and the European starling (*Sturnus vulgaris*) are usually considered undesirable birds. Both species were introduced from Europe and, like occupying armies, have made a very good life here. These hooligans out compete many native birds for prime nesting holes and often exclude smaller native birds from feeders. They are rarely seen far from human habitations, and there is no foolproof way to deter them. However, you can discourage them by using feeders designed to exclude them, such as thistle tubes and satellite feeders, and by avoiding mixed "wild bird" seed.

TREES AND SHRUBS FOR WINTER BIRDS

Happily, the trees and shrubs that draw birds and other animals into our gardens in winter are also those we value for aesthetic reasons year-round, but most particularly in winter.

TABLE 18: TREES AND SHRUBS THAT ATTRACT WINTER BIRDS

Tree	Use
Mountain ash (*Sorbus* spp.)	Berries
Colorado blue spruce (*Picea pungens* f. *glauca*)	Winter protection; seeds
Mugo pine (*Pinus mugo* var. *mugo*)	Cover from predators; seeds
Crabapple (*Malus*) cultivars	Withered fruit
Birch (*Betula* spp.)	Seeds within mature catkins
Aspen and poplar (*Populus* spp.)	Overwintering insects or insect eggs in bark crevices
Caragana (*Caragana*) cultivars	Protection from predators and the wind
Spirea (*Spiraea*) cultivars	Protection from predators
Viburnum or highbush cranberry (*Viburnum* spp.)	Berries
Hawthorn (*Crataegus* spp.)	Protection from predators; fruit

Plant Summaries Explained

The plant characteristics used in this section are defined as follows.

Type: notes whether the recommended plant is an annual, bulb, perennial, or woody ornamental tree, shrub, or vine, and the family to which it belongs.

Winter Features: details the plant's winter values, such as fruit or leaf retention, attractive seed heads, interesting bark, attraction to wildlife, and usefulness for winter arrangements.

Other Features: outlines plant values that are present during the traditional gardening season, such as flowers and leaf color.

Landscape Uses: describes plant use, such as situating in a flower, mixed, or shrub border; hedging, naturalizing, or screening; or as a feature or foundation plant.

Height and Spread: indicates size of typical mature plant; climate varies across the northern prairies and, generally, the harsher the climate, the smaller the plant; microclimate and culture also affect plant size.

Soil: defines fertility and drainage. Fertility is described as poor, average, or fertile. Drainage includes moist or well drained. Moisture-holding capabilities are increased by amending the soil with organics like peat, compost, or well-rotted manure and by applying a 5-cm (2-in.) layer of mulch. In addition to humus, drainage may also be improved in clay soils by adding sharp, coarse sand.

Light: identifies daily plant preference for full sun (eight or more hours), part sun (six to eight hours), part shade (four to six hours), or shade (less than four hours).

Growing Tips: lists salient points for growing the plant, including winter concerns described in Chapter Six.

Alternatives: provides alternative plants to use if the plant is not available in your area or is inappropriate for your garden.

Winter and Summer Density/Texture: notes these characteristics for woody ornamentals in both summer and winter to help you with planning contrast or repetition.

Botanical Names

Both "common" and botanical names are used to refer to plants. Common names vary by locale; one person's saskatoon is another's shadbush or serviceberry. There are at least four different plants called "dusty miller," and few are even slightly related. To get the exact plant you want, shop for it using its botanical name.

Botanical nomenclature is based on a series of classifications. The analogy to people that is used here may help you understand the hierarchy and intent of botanical naming.

Family: like people, plants belong to a certain clan, and you may be surprised at who's in the extended family tree. For example, mountain ash, crabapples, and roses are all members of the family *Rosaceae*.

Genus: the plant equivalent to a person's last name. It's a group of closely related but unique species, for example, *Rosa.*

Species: a specific plant within a genus, the equivalent of a person known by both first and last name, for example, *Rosa rugosa.* A species can breed true from seed. Species and genus are always italicized; the non-italicized abbreviations sp. (singular) and spp. (plural) denote species within a genus.

Varieties and Forms: naturally occurring plants that are very similar to the species but with some noteworthy characteristic, for example, *Rosa rugosa* var. *alba* (white flowering rugosa rose) and *Picea pungens* f. *glauca* (the blue form of the Colorado spruce).

Cultivar: means cultivated variety (requiring human intervention) and is noted in roman type in single quotes, for example, *Rosa* 'Blanc Double de Coubert'.

Hybrid: indicates plants created by cross-breeding species, varieties, forms, and even genera. An "x" denotes a hybrid, for example, *Malus* x *adstringens.*

Ten

Bones, Bark, and Berries—
Deciduous Trees and Shrubs

Berberis thunbergii

(*ber*-ber-is thun-*ber*-gee-ee)

Japanese barberry

Plant at a Glance (*illustration p. 100*)

Type: shrub of the barberry family (*Berberidaceae*)

Winter Features: may retain fruit, colored young bark, spines, retains some leaves

Other Features: yellow flowers, burgundy or yellow leaves, fall color, red or yellow-green berries, attracts bees

Landscape Uses: mixed or shrub border, barrier hedge, feature plant, ground-cover

Height: 0.6 to 1.5 m (2 to 5 ft.)

Spread: 0.6 to 1.5 m (2 to 5 ft.)

Soil: poor to average

Light: full to part sun

Growing Tips: drought tolerant

Winter Density/Texture: medium/medium

Summer Density/Texture: dense/medium-fine

Description

Japanese barberries were banned in both Canada and the United States because certain varieties are disease carriers for black stem rust, a fungus that ruins cereal crops and causes economic hardship in agricultural areas. They were reintroduced to the United States a few decades ago when rust-resistant cultivars were developed and have been reintroduced recently to Canada.

*Japanese barberry (*Berberis thunbergii*) (p. 99)*
NORA BRYAN

Densely clothed in small leaves with foliage colors ranging from purple-red to yellow to green, the barberry shrub offers four seasons of interest. Autumn color depends on the original leaf color and, of course, the type and timing of fall weather. The plants lend themselves to shearing because they have many small leaves.

The red-leafed barberries offer the most winter interest. Tiny, shiny, almost unreal-looking berries are shaped like narrow teardrops or jelly beans. New bark is an arresting red, and the texture added by spines of a similar color makes this a great shrub for the landscape.

Red-leafed cultivars come in a variety of sizes and forms. Compact 'Royal Burgundy' (0.6 by 1 m; 2 by 3 ft.) and 'Concorde' (0.5 by 0.5 m; 1.5 by 1.5 ft.) have slight differences in leaf color. The medium-sized 'Cherry Bomb' (1 by 1 m; 3 by 3 ft.) is a slow-growing red cultivar. 'Rose Glow' (to 1.4 by 1.3 m; 4.5 by 4.25 ft.) is a mounding shrub suitable for hedging. 'Royal Cloak' (to 1.6 by 1.5 m; 5.5 by 5 ft.) has mottled purple-pink foliage and arching branches. The red color intensifies with more sun.

Alternatives

Other shrubs offer purplish foliage, but not as much in terms of winter interest. Purpleleaf sand cherry (*Prunus x cistena*) has purple-toned bark but lacks berries. Some roses like the redleaf rose and 'Thérèse Bugnet' show off their prickles, reddish bark, and fruit in winter. 'Martin Frobisher' also has red canes but lacks rose hips. Turkestan burning bush (*Euonymus nanus* 'Turkestanicus') often will retain many of its deep burgundy-black leaves into winter.

Betula pendula and *B. papyrifera*

(*beh-*tew-lah *pen-*dew-lah and B. pa-pi-*rif-*er-ah)

European white birch and paper birch

Plant at a Glance

Type: tree of the birch family (*Betulaceae*)

Winter Features: white bark with contrasting dark lenticels, architectural form, male catkins, attracts wildlife

Other Features: catkins, yellow fall color

Landscape Uses: feature tree, shade tree

Height: 10 to 15 m (33 to 50 ft.)

Spread: 6 to 10 m (20 to 33 ft.)

Soil: average to fertile, moist, well drained

Light: full sun

Growing Tips: water deeply, especially in fall; prune in summer after leaf-out when sap is no longer running; susceptible to birch leafminer; European birch also susceptible to bronze birch borer

Winter Density/Texture: open/medium-coarse

Summer Density/Texture: medium/medium

Description

Although there are over sixty species of birch, the two most widely seen in prairie gardens are the native paper birch and the larger European white birch. Both have white bark and dark markings, akin to charcoal etchings, and create a breathtaking display against a dark or evergreen background.

Paper birch (*Betula papyrifera*) has an oval to round habit, is relatively fast growing, and is available in both single-stem and clumping form. Native to Canada and the northern United States, it is found near rivers and lakes, performing best where the water table is relatively high. Young bark is smooth and reddish brown; with age, it whitens and peels in horizontal strips like shreds of paper. In winter, the large, white branches have a red-brown aura created by the younger twigs. This halo glows even brighter when covered in hoarfrost. Chickadee birch (*B. papyrifera* 'Chickadee') is a narrow, upright, almost conical paper birch suited to smaller lots. The paper birch

*The white bark of this European birch (*Betula pendula *'Gracilis') contrasts beautifully with the dark spruce.*

NORA BRYAN

is smaller and hardier than the European white birch, but lacks the variety of shapes and forms.

The European white birch (*Betula pendula*) (syn. *B. verrucosa*) grows to 25 by 10 m (82 by 33 ft). Cultivars include the large, fine-textured weeping cultivars 'Laciniata' and 'Gracilis'. 'Trost's Dwarf' has a very unusual form and grows only 1.5 m (5 ft.) tall. Young's weeping European birch (*B. pendula* 'Youngii') can be topped at the preferred height or grown to 8 m (26 ft.) tall. It also comes in a "wavy stem" form for additional winter interest. The stem may not be visible in summer due to the tree's long, pendulous branches.

Alternatives

Other white-barked woody ornamentals include greenish white poplars and aspens (*Populus* spp.) and silver buffaloberry (*Shepherdia argentea*). River or black birch (*Betula nigra*) has dark, peeling bark when mature and light lenticular markings. In clump form, it displays its attractive deep bronze bark.

Caragana arborescens 'Sutherland'

(ka-ra-*gah*-nah ar-bo-*res*-kens)

Sutherland caragana

Plant at a Glance *(illustration p. 104)*

    Type: shrub or tree of the pea family (*Fabaceae*)

    Winter Features: olive green bark, columnar form

    Other Features: yellow pealike flowers, podlike fruit, yellow autumn leaves

    Landscape Uses: mixed border, screening, feature or foundation plant

    Height: 4 to 5 m (13 to 16 ft.)

    Spread: 1 to 1.5 m (3 to 5 ft.)

    Soil: average to poor, well drained

    Light: full to part sun

    Growing Tips: perfect for narrow, hot spots; remove heavy, wet snow from branches; avoid cultivation that could damage roots and cause suckering; trim any suckers from the base

    Winter Density/Texture: medium/medium-coarse

    Summer Density/Texture: medium/medium base

Description

Very hardy *Caragana arborescens* originates in Siberia and prefers cold winters and hot, dry summers. At one time, these caraganas were popular garden shrubs and hedges. When grown on smaller urban lots, species caraganas may display wanton suckering, but this is not an issue with 'Sutherland'.

Sutherland caragana is an upright, salt-tolerant, hardy shrub, with dense, tiny leaves and yellow flowers in spring. The shrub provides winter interest with its bark, a subtle olive green with pale horizontal lenticels, best displayed against lighter or brown backgrounds. Unlike most caraganas, it has few spines. Its columnar form makes a strong point in the winter landscape. Plant it singularly to highlight a feature, in pairs when framing a view or a focal point in a formal setting, or in groups of three or more.

Alternatives

Siberian columnar crabapple (*Malus baccata* 'Columnaris') and columnar mountain ash (*Sorbus aucuparia* 'Fastigiata') also achieve a tall, columnar shape. Swedish columnar aspen (*Populus tremula* 'Erecta') is significantly taller.

Caragana arborescens 'Pendula' and 'Walker'
(ka-ra-*gah*-nah ar-bo-*res*-kens)
Weeping and Walker caragana

Plant at a Glance *(illustration p. 109)*
Type: shrub or dwarf tree of the pea family (*Fabaceae*)
Winter Features: olive green bark, tortuous form
Other Features: yellow pealike flowers, podlike fruit, yellow autumn leaves
Landscape Uses: mixed border, feature plant
Height: 0.6 to 1.5 m (2 to 5 ft.)
Spread: 1 to 1.2 m (3 to 4 ft.)
Soil: poor to average
Light: full to part sun
Growing Tips: drought and heat tolerant once established; tolerates salty and alkaline soil; trim suckers at base of plant
Winter Density/Texture: medium/medium
Summer Density/Texture: dense/medium-coarse

Description

Dwarf weeping plants fit visually in a winter garden; they look slightly tortured and bent over as if huddling into the ground away from cold winds and freezing temperatures.

Weeping caragana is a small shrub with strongly cascading branches. It has leaves like a typical caragana, each comprised of four to six pairs of elliptical leaflets ending in spines. The leaves of the Walker caragana are even narrower and finer, almost fernlike, in texture. In its ungrafted form, weeping or Walker caragana can be planted atop a retaining wall

Sutherland caragana
(Caragana arborescens
'Sutherland') (p. 102)

to soften its line, by allowing the branches to fall over the edge. However, it is usually sold as a small tree, grafted onto a single stem of Sutherland caragana. Its height is somewhat variable, based on the length of the standard (the straight stem) used.

Alternatives

Other dwarf deciduous weeping plants include the Red Jade crabapple (*Malus* x 'Red Jade'), Trost's weeping birch (*Betula pendula* 'Trost's Dwarf'), and weeping European larch (*Larix decidua* 'Pendula'). Weeping European larch (3 to 9 m; 10 to 30 ft. wide) normally creeps along the ground but, if staked, creates an interesting specimen.

Cornus alba 'Sibirica'
(*kor*-nus *all*-bah)
Siberian coral or red-twig dogwood

Plant at a Glance *(illustration p. 157)*
Type: shrub of the dogwood family (*Cornaceae*)
Winter Features: bright red bark, attracts wildlife, winter arrangements
Other Features: white flowers, blue-white berries, reddish autumn leaves
Landscape Uses: mixed or shrub border, mass planting
Height: 2 to 3 m (6.5 to 10 ft.)
Spread: 2 to 3 m (6.5 to 10 ft.)
Soil: poor to average, moist, well drained
Light: full sun to part shade
Growing Tips: mulch; prune out at least 20% of oldest twigs or cut back to ground level after leaf drop for good stem color (the more stems you remove, the fewer flowers and berries produced the following year); leaf and stem color are brighter in full sun and moist soil
Winter Density/Texture: variable/medium-fine
Summer Density/Texture: dense, becoming more open with age/medium-coarse

Description

Siberian dogwood, originating in northern Asia, is cold hardy. This medium-size, round to spreading shrub acts primarily as a backdrop for other plants in summer. White berries tinged with blue follow white flowers. Its leaves, which have a rough texture due to veining, become dull purple-red in autumn as its branches, especially young ones, deepen to a rich red color. In winter, it looks wonderful coupled with evergreens in mass plantings and against light-colored fences and walls.

Cultivars vary in size and leaf coloration, including variegation, adding increased summer interest. The trade-off is that their stems are not as brilliant as those of 'Sibirica'. 'Argenteo-marginata' has leaves outlined in cream, as does the slightly smaller 'Bailhalo' ('Ivory Halo'). Both contrast well with purple-foliaged plants. Cultivars 'Spaethii' and 'Gouchaultii' have leaves with yellow edges, instead of cream; the latter includes a mottle of pink. 'Prairie Fire' has yellowish foliage and intense fall coloration.

Purple-twigged dogwood (*Cornus alba* 'Kesselringii') has purple-black twigs, bronze green leaves, and berries similar to the red-twigged cultivars listed above. It pairs well with the red- or yellow-twigged dogwoods.

Alternatives

Red osier dogwood (*Cornus sericea*) (syn. *C. stolonifera*) is a native dogwood found in moist habitats. As the synonym indicates, it spreads and is useful for naturalization. Fast-growing, medium to round in shape, with a lifespan of 20 to 30 years, the red osier's branches are not quite as red nor its leaves as rough as those of the Siberian dogwood. Several cultivars of red osier dogwood provide yellow- or white-leaf variegation and size variation.

Bud's Yellow dogwood
(Cornus sericea 'Bud's Yellow')
NOHA BRYAN

Cornus 'Bud's Yellow' (syn. *C. sericea*, *C. alba* 'Bud's Yellow')
(*kor*-nus)
Bud's Yellow dogwood

Plant at a Glance
Type: shrub of the dogwood family (*Cornaceae*)
Winter Features: yellow bark, attracts wildlife, winter arrangements
Other Features: yellow-white flowers in spring, blue-white fruit, autumn leaves tinged red to burgundy in sun

Landscape Uses: mixed or shrub border, informal hedge
Height: 1.8 m (2.3 ft.)
Spread: 1.5 m (5 ft.)
Soil: average to fertile, moist
Light: part sun to shade
Growing Tips: mulch; prune out at least 20% of oldest twigs or cut back to ground level after leaf drop for good stem color (the more you remove, the fewer flowers and berries you will have); situate where water collects
Winter Density/Texture: medium-open/medium-coarse
Summer Density/Texture: medium/medium-coarse

Description

Bud's Yellow dogwood has bright greenish gold twigs. During winter, the colorful bark shines in the winter sun and is useful for accent and contrast. Place the shrub in front of evergreens or against dark backgrounds, or pair it with purple-twigged dogwood or other dark-stemmed shrubs.

Alternatives

The yellow-twigged *Cornus sericea* 'Flaviramea' is a similar shrub, but has the disadvantage of being more prone to disease than 'Bud's Yellow'. For a large shrub or tree on large properties, the golden willow (*Salix alba* 'Vitellina') is a good alternative, although it needs plenty of space and water for its wide and shallow rooting pattern. It can be chopped to ground level in the spring to keep its twigs bright yellow and its size in check.

Cotoneaster lucidus (syn. *C. acutifolia*)

(ko-to-nee-*ah*-ster *loo*-si-duss, syn. C. a-kew-tih-*fo*-lee-ah)

Hedge or Peking cotoneaster

Plant at a Glance *(illustration p. 16)*

Type: shrub of the rose family (*Rosaceae*)
Winter Features: architectural form if pruned, blue-black berries, winter arrangements, attracts birds
Other Features: orange-red fall color
Landscape Uses: feature plant, mixed or shrub border, hedging, foundation plant, screening
Height: 2 m (6.5 ft.)
Spread: 2 m (6.5 ft.)
Soil: moist, well drained
Light: full sun to part shade
Growing Tips: prefers full sun; apply iron chelate if chlorotic; adapts to dry soil; prune die-back in spring (approximately one-third of shrub); susceptible to

fireblight, cankers, pear slug, and oystershell scale; plant 30 to 45 cm (12 to 18 in.) apart from center to center for hedges
Winter Density/Texture: dense if pruned (otherwise medium)/medium
Summer Density/Texture: dense/medium

Description

Cotoneaster, correctly pronounced co-TONEY-aster, is often mispronounced as cotton-easter. This reliable prairie standard, often pruned into hedges or shaped for a formal look, has ascending to upright branches with dark green, shiny leaves that are hairy below. The shrub is dense with branches, for a solid winter effect. Flowers are small, light pink, and somewhat inconspicuous. The blue-black berries persist, becoming less noticeable as winter progresses.

Gardeners in warmer areas or with sheltered microclimates and good snow cover may be able to grow other *Cotoneaster* species that produce red berries.

Alternatives

Aronia melanocarpa 'Autumn Magic' (black chokeberry) (1 to 1.8 m; 3 to 6 ft. in height and spread) offers similar berry and fall color. Originating in bogs and peaty areas, black chokeberry prefers moist, acidic soil. The shrub looks best with perennials in front as it is naked from the knees down. Prune tip kill in early spring.

Elaeagnus angustifolia

(el-ee-*ag*-nus an-gus-tee-*fo*-lee-ah)
Russian olive

Plant at a Glance *(illustration p. 109)*

Type: large shrub or small tree of the oleaster family (*Elaeagnaceae*)
Winter Features: retains leaves, attracts wildlife, furrowed, nearly black bark, winter arrangements
Other Features: fragrant but inconspicuous yellow flowers, silver leaves, thorns
Landscape Uses: feature plant, shade tree
Height: 4 to 7 m (13 to 23 ft.)
Spread: 6 to 7 m (20 to 23 ft.)
Soil: poor to average, light, dry conditions
Light: full sun
Growing Tips: tolerates salty and alkaline soils; needs good drainage; performs well on southwest-facing slopes
Winter Density/Texture: medium-open/medium
Summer Density/Texture: medium/medium-fine

Description

Russian olive is a small, low-headed, multi-stemmed, oval tree or shrub with an open canopy. Its long, narrow, silver-gray leaves present a fine texture and offer dramatic contrast to its dark bark. The fruit, like small silver olives, is retained in winter. Although it is one of the last trees to leaf out in spring, Russian olive retains many of its silver leaves well into winter, providing outstanding year-round contrast with conifers. Its open-branching habit appears somewhat tortuous during the deep cold of winter. It has a lifespan of 20 to 30 years, and older bark becomes ridged and furrowed for textural interest. It can suffer die-back shortly after leaf-out due to early frosts, and it is only semi-hardy in the Chinook zone.

Alternatives

Other trees and shrubs that offer a similar silver or white color but less density include birch (*Betula* spp.), poplar and aspen (*Populus* spp.), and silver buffaloberry (*Shepherdia argentea*). If you want dark bark, consider the larger, slow-growing bur oak (*Quercus macrocarpa*).

Hippophae rhamnoides
(hip-*poe*-fae-ee ram-*noy*-deez)
Sea buckthorn

Plant at a Glance *(illustration p. 109)*
Type: large shrub or small tree of the oleaster family (*Elaeagnaceae*)
Winter Features: thorns, retains fruit, attracts wildlife, winter arrangements
Other Features: colorful leaves and abundant, edible, yellow-orange berries on females, spreads by rhizomes
Landscape Uses: naturalizing, shelterbelt, slope stabilization, barrier
Height: 4 to 6 m (13 to 20 ft.)
Spread: 4 to 7 m (13 to 23 ft.)
Soil: poor to average, light, well drained
Light: full sun
Growing Tips: apply mulch and avoid root injury to reduce suckering; can be trained as a tree; both male and female plants are required for fruit; salt and drought tolerant
Winter Density/Texture: dense/medium-coarse
Summer Density/Texture: dense/medium-fine

Description

Sea buckthorn is a large, very hardy shrub native to the steppes of Eurasia, which has naturalized in North America. Round to spreading in shape,

*Russian olive
(*Elaeagnus
angustifolia*)
(p. 107)*
NORA BRYAN

*Sea buckthorn
(*Hippophae
rhamnoides*)
(p. 108)*
NORA BRYAN

*An intriguing variety
of textures and
shapes highlights
this grouping of
hydrangea (*Hydrangea
arborescens
'Annabelle') (p. 110),
weeping caragana
(*Caragana arborescens
'Pendula') (p. 103),
horizontal juniper, and
dwarf Russian almond,
with a backdrop of
Techny cedar (*Thuja
occidentalis 'Techny')
(p. 136).*
NORA BRYAN

*Siberian larch
(*Larix sibirica*)
(p. 111)*
NORA BRYAN

*The architectural
form of this Red Jade
weeping crabapple
(*Malus x 'Red Jade')
(p. 114) is repeated
in winter shadow.*
BARBARA KAM

with ascending branches armed with spines, it has a lifespan of 30 to 40 years. Its outstanding winter feature is the dense and tightly held yellow-orange to bright orange berries produced by female plants on the previous year's shoots. Mass planting will increase the likelihood of fruit production. The edible berries, which chickadees like, are high in vitamins C, E, and A and can be so plentiful that the branches are barely visible. The plant is being considered as a commercial fruit producer.

Alternatives

Silver buffaloberry (*Shepherdia argentea*) has similar characteristics, but female plants have red or yellow berries. Another alternative is the hawthorn. Those sturdy enough for prairie winters (*Crataegus* x *mordenensis*) are small, rounded trees with long spines, sparse red berries, and attractive bark color.

Hydrangea arborescens 'Annabelle'
(hi-*drain*-jee-ah ar-bo-*res*-kens)
Annabelle hydrangea

Plant at a Glance *(illustration p. 109)*
Type: shrub of the hydrangea family (*Hydrangaceae*)
Winter Features: attractive seed heads, winter arrangements
Other Features: flowers in mid- to late summer
Landscape Uses: feature plant, mixed or shrub border
Height: 1 to 1.5 m (3 to 5 ft.)
Spread: 1 to 1.5 m (3 to 5 ft.)
Soil: fertile, moist, well drained
Light: part sun to part shade
Growing Tips: prefers sheltered north or east exposures; water well in fall; flowers and seed heads may require support; cut to 10 cm (4 in.) in early spring; prefers acidic soil, so amend generously with compost; apply iron chelate if chlorotic
Winter Density/Texture: open/coarse
Summer Density/Texture: fairly dense/coarse

Description

Native to eastern North America, this hydrangea is a round to spreading shrub with stiff, ascending, non-branching stems and large, bright green leaves. The large, domed flower heads, comprising many creamy white flowers (florets), are sterile. Due to their size, the flower heads may need support in both summer and winter. Its bloom time makes 'Annabelle' a good shrub for brightening a part-shade border later in the season.

The plant's sterile seed heads provide winter interest, when the creamy white color becomes beige, like aging paper. If it is not in your winter sight lines, harvest the dried blooms for winter arrangements.

Alternatives

Pee Gee hydrangea (*Hydrangea paniculata* 'Grandiflora') is a slightly larger shrub with smaller, pinkish flowers that are conical in shape. Cut stems back to live growth in spring and thin to five or six stems for fewer but larger flowers.

The snowball viburnum (*Viburnum opulus* 'Sterile') (2 by 2 m; 6.5 by 6.5 ft.) has similar pom-pom flower heads and purplish autumn color.

Larix sibirica

(*lay*-ricks sy-*beer*-ih-kah)
Siberian larch

Plant at a Glance *(illustration p. 109)*

Type: deciduous conifer of the pine family (*Pinaceae*)
Winter Features: interesting architectural form, contorted, zigzagging branches, cones
Other Features: soft green needles turn bright gold and drop in autumn
Landscape Uses: feature plant, massing on large properties
Height: 10 to 20 m (33 to 65 ft.)
Spread: 4 to 5 m (13 to 16 ft.)
Soil: moist, well drained
Light: full sun
Growing Tips: prefers full sun; adapts to dry soil
Winter Density/Texture: porous/medium
Summer Density/Texture: medium-dense/medium-fine

Description

Larches are unusual conifers because they drop their leaves in fall. The very hardy Siberian larch turns gold in autumn and a fresh, lively green in spring. It is a relatively fast-growing conical tree with branches that arc downward before ascending. In winter, the small female cones make the branches appear knotted, creating a contorted effect. The bark is gray-brown, becoming grayer and flakier with age. The Siberian larch is more suited to prairie conditions than either the native North American western or eastern larch (*Larix occidentalis* and *L. laricina*, respectively).

The hard-to-find *Larix sibirica* 'Conica' (10 by 3 m; 33 by 10 ft.) is a more slow-growing, uniformly shaped cultivar.

Alternatives

Similar in appearance, European larch (*Larix decidua*) is slightly less hardy and prefers moister and more acidic soils. It offers some interesting cultivars to those with deep pockets or a passion for collecting. 'Pendula' is spreading in habit, or it can be staked to form a weeping tree; its ultimate height and width depend on how it is trained. 'Varied Directions' is slow growing with random branching patterns, making each tree unique. For the collector, there are also several cultivars of the native *L. laricina*, including the dwarf 'Newport Beauty' series.

Malus

(*mah*-lus)
Ornamental crabapple

Plant at a Glance (illustration pp. 29, 109, 152)

Type: tree of the rose family (*Rosaceae*)

Winter Features: flaking bark, architectural form, attracts wildlife, some cultivars retain fruit, winter arrangements

Other Features: spring flowers, small fruit, some cultivars have colored leaves, fall colors are yellow, amber, or burgundy

Landscape Uses: feature tree, screening, mixed or shrub border, shelterbelt

Height: 5 to 8 m (16 to 26 ft.)

Spread: 2 to 8 m (6.5 to 26 ft.)

Soil: average to fertile, moist, well drained

Light: full to part sun

Growing Tips: full sun brings more flowers and fruit and intensifies leaf color in those with non-green leaves; drought tolerant once established; prefers slightly acidic soil; water well in early spring; prune to remove crossing branches; choose rust- and fireblight-resistant cultivars

Winter Density/Texture: medium/medium-coarse

Summer Density/Texture: medium to dense/medium-coarse

Description

The crabapple offers four seasons of interest, including spring flowers, interesting form, leaf color variation, yellow or red autumn foliage (depending on original leaf color), interesting bark texture, and, if chosen properly, persistent fruit to provide interest and food for wildlife. A few branches can be pruned after leaf drop to add to winter arrangements.

There are many cultivars of crabapples. Forms include upright ovals, broad spreads, and narrow, columnar fans, while branches may be ascending, arching, or weeping. Leaf color varies from green to bronze to deep purple, while flowers may be single or double, ranging in color from white to pink to purple. The crabapple is a relatively low-headed tree, which means that the branches begin low on the trunk, so it's not suitable near a deck or path unless you like to duck. The small size of most crabapple trees makes it a good choice for urban lots. Most crabapples survive from about 20 to 25 years on the prairies, and as the tree ages, the bark grays and develops flakes and deepening crevices. In shelterbelts, they provide food for birds and squirrels and may be browsed by deer and hares. How long a cultivar holds its fruit into winter depends on frost timing (early killing frosts can turn fruit to mush that drops easily), the autumn insect population (low numbers can cause birds to turn to the crabapples earlier), and the number of birds.

The two main divisions of ornamental crabapples are the rosyblooms and the white-flowering crabapples.

Rosyblooms *(Malus x adstringens)*

Rosyblooms are named for their pink-toned flowers, fruit, and bark. Several hardy cultivars retain their fruit into winter. 'Kelsey' (5.5 by 5.5 m; 18 by 18 ft.) has a round form, double, dark pink flowers, and persistent red-purple fruit. 'Red Splendor' (7.5 by 7 m; 25 by 23 ft.) is a round tree with ascending branches and abundant, persistent red berries. Green-red leaves become red in autumn. 'Rudolph' (5 by 4 m; 16 by 13 ft.) has glossy red-green leaves, red-pink flowers, and red fruit on ascending to arching branches. 'Selkirk' (6 by 7 m; 20 by 23 ft.) has relatively large, pink flowers, green-bronze leaves, and persistent, shiny red fruit. 'Thunderchild' (7.5 by 7.5 m; 25 by 25 ft.) is round in form with dark purple leaves, purple-red fruit, and deep purple bark. Given its dark leaves, fruit is not apparent until leaf drop.

'Morning Princess' and 'Royal Beauty' (5 by 3 m; 16 by 10 ft.) are two purple-leafed weeping crabapple cultivars with lovely winter form that make excellent specimen plants. Control their final height by either bending the leader downward or topping.

White-flowering Crabapples

White-flowering crabapples are very cold hardy and floriferous. Most ornamental and edible crabapples and apples have the Siberian crabapple

(*Malus baccata*) in their parentage for hardiness. They tend to have smaller fruit than the rosyblooms, their green leaves turn gold in fall, and their bark has orange undertones.

White-flowering crabapples have green leaves and single, white flowers. Siberian columnar crabapple (*Malus baccata* 'Columnaris') (6 by 2 m; 20 by 6.5 ft.) is a very narrow, columnar tree well suited to areas with limited tree space. The strongly upright branches can be damaged by early spring or late fall snowfalls when the plants are entering or leaving dormancy, so shake off snow. The abundant small fruit ranges in color from yellow to orange-red.

Rosthern columnar crabapple (*Malus baccata* 'Rosthern') (5.5 by 2.5 m; 18 by 8 ft.) is a narrow, upright oval tree, becoming round with age, with abundant small, orange-red, persistent fruit. Rosthern is less susceptible to fireblight than the narrower Siberian columnar crabapple.

Red Jade crabapple (*Malus* x 'Red Jade') (3.6 by 3.6 m; 12 by 12 ft.) is a green-leafed weeping crabapple with small, shiny red fruit. It is less hardy than the other two white-flowering ornamentals.

With something so good, there has to be a downside. Crabapples can suffer from rust (p. 43), apple maggots, sunscald, apple scab, and fireblight. But don't panic. As part of your pest and disease management program, choose cultivars bred for disease resistance, which includes the majority of newer cultivars.

Alternatives

For four seasons of interest, look to mountain ash (*Sorbus* spp.) for flowering, fruiting, fall color, and various forms.

Populus tremula 'Erecta'

(*pop*-ewe-lus *trem*-ewe-lah)
Swedish columnar aspen

Plant at a Glance *(illustration p. 116)*

Type: shrub or tree of the willow family (*Salicaceae*)
Winter Features: attracts wildlife, architectural form
Other Features: amber autumn leaves
Landscape Uses: screening, feature plant, mixed or shrub border, view framing
Height: 10 to 15 m (33 to 50 ft.)
Spread: 2 to 3 m (6.5 to 10 ft.)
Soil: poor to average, well drained

Light: full to part sun
Growing Tips: to reduce likelihood of suckering, plant the trunk flare at ground level and avoid cultivation around the roots
Winter Density/Texture: open to medium/medium
Summer Density/Texture: dense/medium

Description

Poplars and aspens (*Populus* spp.), two of the few native deciduous trees of the northern prairies, are found in streambeds and along riverbanks. They live life fast and die young. As they age, they increase in value for birds, offering nesting cavities and usually an abundance of insect food in their creviced bark.

Swedish columnar aspens offered for sale are male clones, which, unlike the females, do not produce poplar fluff. Bronze-green leaves emerge in spring before turning dark green. Like most poplars, this tree has greenish white bark with smooth, horizontal lenticels, but it is extremely narrow relative to its height, with branches that are very upright. Early and late snowfalls that occur when the tree is entering or leaving dormancy can cause branches to break.

The dramatic form of these aspens makes a statement in any season. They look fabulous fronting tall spruce, or with junipers or mounding shrubs at their feet.

Alternatives

The Tower poplar (*Populus* x *canescens* 'Tower') is another very tall and narrow poplar, but its branches are wavier, start lower on the trunk, and tend to twist at the top. Its leaves, which have a whitish underside, are more triangular and sharply pointed than those of the Swedish columnar aspen. The Tower poplar also tends to sucker more than the Swedish columnar aspen.

Prunus maackii

(*proo*-nus *mahk*-ee-ee)
Amur cherry, Manchurian cherry

Plant at a Glance *(illustration pp. 29, 128)*
Type: tree of the rose family (*Rosaceae*)
Winter Features: shiny, bronze, exfoliating bark with horizontal lenticels, architectural form

Other Features: abundant small, cream flowers in spring, light yellow leaves in autumn, small black cherries attract birds in mid-summer

Landscape Uses: feature plant

Height: 10 to 12 m (33 to 40 ft.)

Spread: 8 to 10 m (26 to 33 ft.)

Soil: fertile, moist, well drained

Light: full sun

Growing Tips: susceptible to frost crack, so screen or wrap young trunks; may need pruning to remove weak branches; may not be hardy in zone 2; apply iron chelate if chlorotic

Winter Density/Texture: open to medium/medium-coarse

Summer Density/Texture: dense/medium-coarse

Swedish columnar aspen
(Populus tremula 'Erecta')
(p. 114)
BARBARA KAM

Description

Native to northeastern China, this quick-growing and relatively short-lived tree comes in both single-stem and multi-stemmed forms. Its branching may begin somewhat close to the ground; it can be left shrublike or pruned as a tree. It is an upright, oval-shaped tree with off-white flowers borne in bottlebrush clusters. Birds appreciate the small black cherries. Leaves turn light yellow in autumn. Its small size makes the tree suitable for small lots.

The Amur cherry has peeling, shiny copper bark with lighter horizontal markings called lenticels. Its bark and overall form make the tree an attractive feature in the winter garden. The clump form makes a stronger winter statement, due to the bark mass at eye level.

Alternatives

Pin cherry (*Prunus pensylvanica*) (8 by 6 m; 26 by 20 ft.) has shiny, green leaves, which become amber or red in fall, white flowers, red fruit, and shiny, purple-bronze bark with horizontal lenticels. The fruit, however, is not retained through the winter. 'Jumping Pound' is a weeping form that grows to 4 m (13 ft.) tall; 'Mary Liss' has larger fruit, and 'Stockton' has double flowers. Nanking cherry (*P. tomentosa*) is a shrub with horizontally exfoliating bark.

Mountain ash (*Sorbus* spp.) also has bronze bark, cream flowers, and persistent orange berries.

Japanese tree lilac (*Syringa reticulata*) and the cultivar 'Ivory Silk' are small trees available in both single-stem and clump form. Young bark is an attractive purple-brown with lighter horizontal lenticels. As the bark matures, it cracks and scales.

Rosa glauca and R. rugosa

(*ros*-ah *glaw*-ah and R. *roo*-*go*-sah)
Redleaf and rugosa rose

Plant at a Glance (*illustration p. 36*)

Type: shrub of the rose family (*Rosaceae*)

Winter Features: retains hips, attracts wildlife, winter arrangements

Other Features: flowers, colorful leaves, prickles

Landscape Uses: mixed or shrub border, barrier hedge, foundation plant

Height: to 3 m (10 ft.) for R. glauca; 1.5 to 2.5 m (5 to 8 ft.) for R. rugosa

Spread: to 2 m (6.5 ft.) for R. glauca; 1.5 to 2.5 m (5 to 8 ft.) for R. rugosa

Soil: average to fertile, well drained

Light: full to part sun

Growing Tips: apply generous compost mulch annually in spring; prune dieback to an outfacing bud in spring; water with soaker hoses to reduce spread of black spot, rust, and mildew; rugosa roses may need treatment with iron chelate

Winter Density/Texture: fairly open/coarse

Summer Density/Texture: dense/coarse

Description

Some of the best roses for hips are species roses—those that occur naturally without human-driven hybridization. These roses have single flowers and bloom only once each summer, but they offer four seasons of interest. The roses look wonderful rising from just behind horizontal junipers.

Two of the best species for winter interest in urban plantings are the redleaf rose (*Rosa glauca*) (syn. *R. rubrifolia*) and the rugosa rose (*R. rugosa*).

The redleaf rose has arching, purple-red canes and ferny, glaucous blue-green leaves. It is often grown more for its foliage than its flowers, which are borne in profusion once in spring. Blooms have five bubblegum-pink petals surrounding yellow stamens. Later, oval, orange-brown hips contrast well with the waxy-looking, dark purple winter stem color.

The rugosa rose is so named for the rough, crinkly texture of its glossy green leaves. A spreading shrub, its flowers range from purple-red to white. The large, orange-red hips may be up to 2.5 cm (1 in.) in size. Single-flowering forms tend to produce the most hips, which are loved by birds, look spectacular on the shrub, and make attractive additions to winter arrangements.

Rose cultivars with *Rosa rugosa* in their parentage also produce hips for winter interest, although not as many as the species, and they have more significant and longer bloom periods in summer. Old prairie favorites like 'Blanc Double de Coubert', 'Hansa', and 'Thérèse Bugnet' have the rugosa rose in their parentage. Other good fruiting cultivars include 'Frau Dagmar Hastrup', 'Dart's Dash', and the Dwarf Pavement series, particularly 'Hanbau' (pink) and 'Uhlensch' (white) cultivars. The Explorer series of roses has rugosa parents, so most will produce some hips; 'Martin Frobisher' will not, but offers red canes instead.

Since rugosa rose cultivars have a tendency to be naked from the knees down, cover their bare legs with perennials that are from 0.3 to 0.6 m (1 to 2 ft.) tall. For cultivars that bloom more than once, regular deadheading extends the bloom period. Stop deadheading a month before the expected killing frost date in your area to allow hip formation.

Alternatives

The Altai rose (*Rosa spinosissima* 'Altaica') (syn. *R. pimpinellifolia* 'Grandiflora') (2.5 by 2 m; 8 by 6.5 ft.) is very hardy, with scented, large, single white flowers in early summer followed by large, purple-black hips. It has gray-green foliage and very prickly branches, and it can sucker. The Scotch Briar rose (*R. spinosissima*) (syn. *R. pimpinellifolia*) is similar, but grows only to 1 m (3 ft.) tall and has creamier-colored flowers.

Salix

(*say*-licks)

Willow

Plant at a Glance (*illustration p. 120*)

Type: shrub or tree of the willow family (*Salicaceae*)

Winter Features: ridged old bark, colorful young bark, attracts wildlife

Other Features: spring catkins

Landscape Uses: (shrubs) mixed or shrub border, hedges, naturalizing; (trees) screening, feature plant, shelterbelt

Height: 1 to 15 m (3 to 50 ft.)

Spread: 1 to 15 m (3 to 50 ft.)

Soil: poor to fertile, moist

Light: full to part shade

Growing Tips: shade and drought intolerant; prefers sandy soils along riverbanks

Winter Density/Texture: medium to dense/coarse

Summer Density/Texture: dense/coarse

Description

Willows are shallow-rooted, fast-growing trees and shrubs with long, lance-shaped leaves. Their wood is brittle and can break from wind and snow. Large willows are primarily suited to acreages and shelterbelts; smaller willows are suitable for urban yards. All but the smallest willows provide shelter for birds. The following willows offer additional winter interest.

Large Willows

Redstem willow (*Salix alba* 'Chermesina') (to 15 by 15 m; 50 by 50 ft.) is round to spreading in habit. New twigs are red-orange.

Golden willow (*Salix alba* 'Vitellina') (to 15 by 15 m; 50 by 50 ft.) has bright yellow, young stems that look stunning against the blue prairie sky.

Laurel-leaf willow (*Salix pentandra*) (to 15 by 15 m; 50 by 50 ft.) is often multi-stemmed or very low headed. Glossy, dark green leaves are held into autumn, and bark becomes deeply furrowed with age. It can be chlorotic in highly alkaline soils.

The hybrid *Salix* x 'Prairie Cascade' (12 by 10.5 m; 40 by 35 ft.) has a weeping form in summer. In winter, its shape is less pendulous but still unusual. Its new twigs are yellow. It can be difficult to establish in colder or Chinook areas, dying back to the snowline.

The bark of old, large willows is deeply creviced, offering many over-wintering insects as food to birds such as chickadees and nuthatches.

Willow (Salix sp.)
(p. 119).
NORA BRYAN

The golden-twigged cultivar of
the white willow tree (Salix alba
'Vitellina') can be coppiced annually
to keep it shrub sized (p. 119).
NORA BRYAN

Small Willows

Both *Salix alba* 'Vitellina' and 'Chermesina' can be grown as tall shrubs if coppiced (pruned to ground level) periodically.

Flame willow (*Salix* x 'Flame') (to 6 by 4 m; 20 by 13 ft.) ranges in size from a medium shrub to a small tree. It has an oval shape and its branches, which are orange-red in winter, curl up and inward. Flame willow has long-lasting, gold autumn-leaf coloration. It pairs well with cedars and is less susceptible to wind damage than other willows.

Purple osier willows (*Salix purpurea* 'Gracilis') and the dwarf 'Nana' (to 1 by 1 m; 3 by 3 ft.) are similarly sized on the prairies due to die-back. Treat them as herbaceous perennials and cut them back in spring. Their purplish stems add winter interest.

Marquette pussy willow (*Salix* x 'Marquette') (to 5 by 5 m; 16 by 16 ft.) has reddish twigs and lots of catkins.

Silver buffaloberry
(Shepherdia argentea*)*
NORA BRYAN

Alternatives

For colorful bark, check out dogwood shrubs (*Cornus* spp.) and certain roses (*Rosa* spp.).

Shepherdia argentea
(shep-*ur*-dee-ah ar *jen*-tee-ah)
Silver buffaloberry

Plant at a Glance

Type: shrub of the oleaster family (*Elaeagnaceae*)

Winter Features: retains fruit, attracts wildlife, winter arrangements

Other Features: silver leaves, spiny stems, spreads by rhizomes

Landscape Uses: naturalizing, slope stabilization, shelterbelt, feature plant when pruned as a tree

Height: 3 to 5 m (10 to 16 ft.)

Spread: 2 to 2.5 m (6.5 to 8 ft.)

Soil: poor to average

Light: full to part sun

Growing Tips: drought tolerant; both male and female plants are required for fruit production; can be pruned into a small accent tree; apply mulch and avoid root injury to reduce suckering

Winter Density/Texture: medium/medium

Summer Density/Texture: dense/medium-fine

Description

Silver buffaloberry is native to the southern portion of the prairies through to Kansas and Nevada. It has lovely narrow, silver foliage on thorny branches, with an overall irregularly round shape. In winter, the texture is coarser and more open with an irregular, twisted branching habit. Its lifespan is 40 to 50 years. The mass of bright red berries along the branches of female shrubs is its outstanding winter feature, although even the tiny, white clusters of male flower buds are attractive in winter. Mass planting will increase the likelihood of setting berries. In containers, the silver stems and round floral buds or berries provide interesting contrast to evergreens. *Shepherdia argentea* 'Goldeye' has yellow fruit.

Alternatives

Sea buckthorn (*Hippophae rhamnoides*) is another silver-leafed shrub that holds its berries well into winter.

Sorbaria sorbifolia
(sor-*bear*-ee-ah sor-be-*fo*-lee-ah)
Ural false spirea

Plant at a Glance *(illustration p. 124)*

Type: shrub of the rose family (*Rosaceae*)
Winter Features: attractive seed heads, winter arrangements
Other Features: late-summer cream flower clusters, spreads by rhizomes
Landscape Uses: naturalizing, tall groundcover
Height: 2 m (6.5 ft.)
Spread: 1.2 to 1.5 m (4 to 5 ft.)
Soil: moist, well drained
Light: full sun to part shade
Growing Tips: prefers moist, sunny sites but will grow in dry shade with less vigor; susceptible to red spider mite in drier conditions
Winter Density/Texture: variable/medium-coarse
Summer Density/Texture: variable/medium-fine

Description

As the botanical name *Sorbaria sorbifolia* suggests, Ural false spirea's leaves resemble those of a mountain ash, giving this shrub a fernlike appearance. The flowers are large, creamy panicles. Deep cinnamon seed heads look like a cross between those of astilbe and lilac. This fast-growing shrub spreads by rhizomes and its overall shape is round to spreading, with strongly ascending, hollow branches. The density of the shrub varies based on cultural conditions; Ural false spirea is denser in moister, sunnier sites than in drier shade. The plant's tendency to sucker makes it suitable for acreages and enclosed areas of urban settings. It works well for woodland and natural style gardens.

The cultivar *Sorbaria* x *hybrida* 'Aurora' has a vigorous spreading habit that is useful for soil stabilization, but is too invasive for most urban lots.

Alternatives

Two perennials—taller astilbe cultivars and goatsbeard—offer plumelike seed heads similar in look to Ural false spirea. Goatsbeard (*Aruncus dioicus*) grows in relatively dry shade and may reach a height and spread similar to Ural false spirea's, but does not sucker. Since the seed heads of these two alternatives are on herbaceous instead of woody stems, they may need to be established to provide a winter show and may not persist as long.

Spring-blooming, white-flowering spirea shrubs offer the "fluffiness" of Ural false spirea's red-brown seed heads without the plume shape. They range in height from 1 to 2.5 m (3 to 8 ft.). Consider bridal wreath spirea (*Spiraea* x *vanhouttei*), garland spirea (*S.* x *arguta*), and three-lobed spirea (*S. trilobata*).

Sorbus americana, S. aucuparia, and S. decora

(*sore*-bus ah-mare-ee-*kan*-ah, S. ah-kewe-*pare*-ee-ah, S. day-*kor*-ah)

Mountain ash

Plant at a Glance *(illustration pp. 29, 125)*

Type: tree of the rose family (*Rosaceae*)

Winter Features: retains fruit, shiny copper brown bark, attracts wildlife, winter arrangements, architectural form

Other Features: small, white clusters of flowers, orange to red berries in clusters begin in late summer, orange to red autumn color

Landscape Uses: feature plant, mixed border

Height: 5 to 8 m (16 to 26 ft.)

Spread: 5 to 8 m (16 to 26 ft.)

Soil: average to fertile, moist, well drained

Light: full to part sun

Growing Tips: susceptible to sunscald, so screen or wrap young trunks; do not plant in a low-lying area with poor drainage; choose fireblight- and rust-resistant cultivars

Winter Density/Texture: variable/medium-coarse

Summer Density Texture: variable/medium-fine

Description

Mountain ash is a valuable tree for a small urban lot, providing four seasons of interest with flowers, berries, fall color, and beautiful bark. It is available in both single-stem and multi-stem forms. In spring, clusters of white to off-white flowers decorate the tree. Orange or red berries, loved by birds, follow in late summer and are conspicuous against the dark green leaves. In fall, the tree is ablaze in orange and red, camouflaging the berries. When the foliage drops, the smooth, shiny copper bark is on view and the berries are again visible.

Of the three species commonly available on the prairies, showy mountain ash (*Sorbus decora*) (6 to 8 by 5 m; 20 to 26 by 16 ft.) is smaller and longer flowering, and has larger berries than the other two species. 'Grootendorst' is a same-sized, fireblight-resistant cultivar. American mountain ash (*S. americana*) (8 by 6 m; 26 by 20 ft.) is also fireblight resistant. The slightly less hardy European mountain ash or rowan (*S. aucuparia*) (9 by 7 m; 30 by 23 ft.) has orange rather than red fruit. Its leaves may not develop fall color in years with early killing frosts.

In its favor, the European mountain ash has many cultivars, including some with unusual forms. The columnar 'Fastigiata' (8 by 2.5 m; 26 by 8 ft.) is sometimes recommended in place of the Siberian columnar crabapple as it is more resistant to fireblight. The weeping 'Pendula' is shorter and wide spreading. 'Rossica' (8 by 4 m; 26 by 13 ft.) is a narrow, oval shape with strongly erect branches and leaves that persist into late autumn; it is more fireblight resistant than the species. The somewhat-columnar 'Black Hawk' and

Ural false spirea
(Sorbaria sorbifolia)
(p. 122)
BARBARA KAM

the red-berried 'Cardinal Royal' (syn. 'Michred') (11 by 6 m; 36 by 20 ft.) are two other available cultivars.

Alternatives

Other trees offering as many seasonal features as mountain ash include some of the ornamental crabapple cultivars (*Malus*), Amur cherry (*Prunus maackii*), pin cherry (*P. pensylvanica*), and, to a lesser extent, Japanese lilac tree (*Syringa reticulata*).

Spiraea x bumalda

(spy-*ree*-ah x boo-*mall*-dah)

Rose blooming spirea

Plant at a Glance *(illustration p. 44)*

Type: shrub of the rose family (*Rosaceae*)

Winter Features: attractive red-brown seed heads, often retains leaves, reddish brown twigs

Other Features: long flowering with pink blooms, some cultivars have colorful leaves, attracts bees

Landscape Uses: feature plant, mixed or shrub border, hedging, foundation plant

Height: 0.6 to 1 m (2 to 3 ft.)

Spread: 0.6 to 1 m (2 to 3 ft.)

Soil: well drained, moist

Light: full sun to part shade

Growing Tips: prefers full sun, especially yellow-leafed cultivars; apply iron chelate if chlorotic; does not tolerate wet soil; adapts to dry soil; prune die-back

*The classic combination of Bark and berries of mountain ash (*Sorbus spp.*) glow under the blue prairie sky (p. 123).*
NORA BRYAN

*Highbush cranberry (*Viburnum trilobum*) (p. 126)*
NORA BRYAN

in spring (approximately one-third of shrub); may self-sow if seed heads left in winter
Winter Density/Texture: quite dense/medium-fine
Summer Density/Texture: dense/medium-fine

Description

This fast-growing, round to spreading shrub blooms in summer with pink flowers on new wood. Flowers are borne in a profusion of flat-topped clusters, which become red-brown seed heads. The shrub is dense with branches for a solid winter effect. The cultivar 'Goldflame' has yellowish leaves, becoming copper orange in autumn. The leaves of 'Anthony Waterer', 'Dart's Red', 'Froebelii', and 'Crispa' turn various shades of purple in fall.

Spring-blooming, white-flowering spireas also have red-brown seed heads, but as they bloom earlier, many of the seed heads may have dispersed. They range in height from 1 to 2.5 m (3 to 8 ft.) and can be round to spreading, with either ascending or arching branches. Consider bridal wreath spirea (*Spiraea* x *vanhouttei*), garland spirea (*S.* x *arguta*), and three-lobed spirea (*S. trilobata*).

Japanese spirea (*Spiraea japonica*) is slightly less hardy than the rose blooming spirea and begins blooming about a week later. Cultivars include the yellow-leafed 'Goldmound' and 'Shirobana', which produces both pink and white flowers.

Alternatives

Choose the prairie-hardy potentilla for similar winter density, shape, and size, but with a tousled, less formal look. These plants will self-sow but their dense, round to oval shape is an attractive foil to creeping junipers or open mugo pines.

Viburnum trilobum
(vy-*bur*-num try-*lo*-bum)
American highbush cranberry

Plant at a Glance *(illustration p. 125)*
Type: shrub of the honeysuckle family (*Caprifoliaceae*)
Winter Features: retains fruit, attracts wildlife, winter arrangements
Other Features: white spring flowers, fall color
Landscape Uses: large mixed or shrub border, hedge
Height: 2 to 4 m (6.5 to 13 ft.)
Spread: 2 to 4 m (6.5 to 13 ft.)

Soil: moist, well drained

Light: full sun to part shade

Growing Tips: mulch shallow roots; full sun promotes flower creation and intensifies autumn coloration; hose off aphids

Winter Density/Texture: medium/medium

Summer Density/Texture: medium/coarse

Description

The American highbush cranberry is a very hardy, round to spreading shrub with ascending branches and dark green leaves. Showy white, flat-topped clusters of flowers are borne in late spring. Plant two varieties of cranberry to ensure cross-pollination for setting fruit. Many of these flower clusters become bright red, translucent berries, reminiscent of round jellybeans glowing in the sun. Play up the young, reddish twigs by pairing them with evergreens or wall colors. The edible fruit attracts deer, fox, pheasants, and other wildlife. For those gardening in semi-natural areas, consider how far you want to invite certain animals into your "groomed" space when choosing this plant.

Viburnum trilobum 'Compactum' (syn. 'Bailey's Compact') is slightly smaller at 1.5 to 2 m (5 to 6.5 ft.) wide and round. Its branching habit is more consistently upright, giving it a somewhat formal winter appearance. *V. trilobum* 'Wentworth' produces larger and more fruit, benefiting both birds and the winter landscape.

Prune some of the older branches to ground level immediately after blooming to allow next year's buds to form or forgo next year's buds for this year's berries in your winter containers.

Alternatives

Nannyberry or sweet viburnum (*Viburnum lentago*) is a large, oval shrub, 3 to 6 m (10 to 20 ft.) tall by 2 to 3 m (6.5 to 10 ft.) wide, with dark, shiny green leaves and deep red autumn color. Its berry clusters start out red and turn deep blue, almost black. On the eastern prairies, downy arrow-wood (*V. rafinesquianum*) is a medium-small shrub with white flower clusters, purple fall foliage, and persistent black fruit. It is not readily available and is prone to tip kill. Wayfaring tree (*V. lantana*) is another large shrub with white flower clusters and fruit that changes from red to black. It has purple-red fall foliage. *V. opulus* 'Nanum' seldom produces fruit, although the species does.

An arbor provides a focal point for Rocky Mountain juniper (Juniperus scopulorum cultivars) (p. 130), mugo pine (p. 133), Amur cherry (Prunus maackii) (p. 115), and a globe blue spruce (p. 132). Trunk wrapping prevents sunscald on the exposed Amur cherry.
NORA BRYAN

Eleven

Queen of the Green— Evergreen Conifers

Juniperus sabina
(yoo-*nip*-er-us sah-*bee*-nah)

Savin juniper

Plant at a Glance *(illustration p. 44)*

Type: shrub of the cypress family (*Cupressaceae*)
Winter Features: evergreen, attracts wildlife, winter arrangements
Other Features: brown-blue pseudo-berries are actually cones
Landscape Uses: groundcover, mixed or shrub border, foundation plant, massing
Height: 0.3 to 2 m (1 to 6.5 ft.) or taller
Spread: 1.8 to 3 m (6 to10 ft.) or wider
Soil: poor to average, well drained
Light: full to part sun
Growing Tips: can be sheared for a formal cut edge or pruned back to an up-growing (rather than side-branching) "leaf" for a more natural look; alternate host with rose family member for various rusts (see p. 43); drought tolerant
Winter Density/Texture: dense/medium-fine
Summer Density/Texture: dense/medium-fine

Description

Savin junipers are native to northern Eurasian mountainous regions and come in a variety of heights. Relatively slow growing, their ascending branches present a wide, vase shape. The species and earlier-developed cultivars tend to be larger and coarser in appearance than newer alternatives. Today, there is plenty of choice in both size and color.

Bright green 'Buffalo' and 'Calgary Carpet' are two of the smaller cultivars (0.3 by 2.5 m; 1 ft. by 8 ft.), giving a bushier look than horizontal junipers of similar dimensions. 'Blue Danube' grows to 1 m (3 ft.) in height and is a dull blue-green.

Savins are good choices for winter interest due to their height and elegant branching habit. Their rich green or bluish color also makes a contrasting carpet for red-twigged plants or those with orange bark. Surround young junipers with low-growing perennial groundcovers like snow-in-summer or creeping bellflower; the spreading junipers will eventually smother the perennials.

Alternatives

The less-hardy pfitzer juniper (*Juniperus* x *pfitzeriana*) (syn. *J.* x *media*) cultivars also can be used as medium-tall groundcovers, although their branching habit is more horizontal than that of the savin. Gold-tipped cultivar 'Aurea' is even less hardy and can suffer die-back when temperatures fall below -35°C (-31°F). 'Goldcoast' is slightly hardier.

Common juniper (*J. communis*) presents a vase shape like the savin and can grow to 2 m (6.5 ft.) tall. Its yellow cultivar 'Depressa Aurea' is hardier than the pfitzer.

Taller cultivars of the faster-growing horizontal juniper (*Juniperus horizontalis*) like 'Andorra' and 'Hughes' may work in winter. Because branches grow horizontally, snow tends to blanket the shrub rather than surround the branches. Shorter cultivars present rippling ground texture when blanketed, but only provide color in areas with limited snow cover, whether from low precipitation or winds.

Juniperus scopulorum
(yoo-*nip*-er-us skop-ewe-*lo*-rum)
Rocky Mountain juniper

Plant at a Glance (illustration p. 128)

Type: large shrub or small tree of the cypress family (*Cupressaceae*)
Winter Features: evergreen, attracts wildlife, winter arrangements, architectural form
Other Features: berries that are actually cones, architectural form even in summer
Landscape Uses: mixed or shrub border, hedge, screening, feature plant, grouping
Height: 3.6 to 8 m (12 to 26 ft.)
Spread: 2 to 5 m (6.5 to 16 ft.)

Soil: poor to average, well drained

Light: full to part sun

Growing Tips: relatively drought tolerant, but requires deep watering until established; brush heavy snow off branches or support branches with net lighting; host to cedar-apple rust (see p. 43); may be affected by spider mites in dry areas

Winter Density/Texture: dense/medium-fine

Summer Density/Texture: dense/medium-fine

Description

A North American native that likes rocky or sandy soil, the Rocky Mountain juniper originated on the eastern slopes of its namesake and can also be found in the badlands of the northern states. Some excellent cultivars originate in North and South Dakota.

These junipers are upright evergreens that are strongly columnar to pyramidal in shape. Some cultivars are very narrow and tightly branched, while others are broader and more open in form. The more open the form, the more coarse textured the plant appears. They range in color from bright green to silver-blue to green-gray.

'Medora' (5 by 2.5 m; 16 by 8 ft.) is one of the hardiest cultivars, with a narrow, columnar form and blue-green color. 'Wichita Blue' (6 by 5 m; 20 by 16 ft.) is a broad, open, bluish cultivar that is much less formal in appearance. Shearing is often recommended to maintain its pyramidal shape. If you do not want an open form, it's less work to select a more appropriate cultivar. 'Gray Gleam' (4 by 1.8 m; 13 by 6 ft.) is a short, narrow, silver cone. The unusual 'Tolleson's Weeping' (6 by 3 m; 20 by 10 ft.) appears somewhat tropical, with its pendulous, silvery green or silvery blue foliage evocative of Spanish moss.

Rocky Mountain junipers partner well with dogwood, are well anchored by horizontal, common, or savin junipers, and provide a foil to berried shrubs and the red-brown abundant seed heads of both spring- and summer-blooming spirea and potentilla.

Alternatives

Other columnar and conical evergreens of similar size include the Brandon and Siberian cedar (*Thuja occidentalis* 'Brandon' and 'Wareana') for sheltered, moist settings. Columnar blue and Montgomery blue spruce (*Picea pungens* f. *glauca* 'Fastigiata' and 'Montgomery') or columnar Scots pine (*Pinus sylvestris* 'Fastigiata') provide evergreen columnar form in sunnier areas.

Picea pungens f. *glauca*
(py-*see*-ah *pun*-jenz f. *glau*-kah)
Colorado blue spruce

Plant at a Glance *(illustration pp. 13, 44, 49, 128)*
   Type: shrub of the pine family (*Pinaceae*)
   Winter Features: evergreen, attracts wildlife, winter arrangements, architectural form
   Other Features: cones
   Landscape Uses: feature plant, shrub border, background plant in rock garden for dwarf cultivars, windscreen
   Height: 1.5 to 4 m (5 to 13 ft.) for dwarf cultivars; to 30 m (100 ft.) for species
   Spread: 1.5 to 2.5 m (5 to 8 ft.) for dwarf cultivars; to 15 m (50 ft.) for species
   Soil: average to fertile, moist, well drained
   Light: full to part sun
   Growing Tips: drought tolerant when established; mulch to just beyond dripline; don't remove lower branches; buy the blue you like, as needle color will not change
   Winter Density/Texture: dense/medium
   Summer Density/Texture: dense/medium

Description

Native to the southern Rockies, the Colorado blue spruce is a form of the green Colorado spruce that has a bluish cast to its needles.

Many true dwarf cultivars come from "witch's brooms" (a top or branch that has developed a deviant form), which must be vegetatively propagated to produce the same plant as the original. Other cultivars are merely slow growing and after many years may outgrow their spot. 'Saint Mary's Broom' is a true dwarf cultivar from a witch's broom, usually only available from specialty nurseries.

Dwarf cultivars of spruce occasionally revert to their much-larger parent form. Telltale signs of reversion are very long new growth on the leader and branch tips, and if imagined over several years, it is clear that the tree will exceed dwarf size. If this happens, either send the tree to someone with a large lot or top it to prevent it from reaching 12 m (40 ft.) high. Snap new growth, called candles, in half each year to maintain its small size.

Globe blue spruce (*Picea pungens* f. *glauca* 'Globosa') (1.5 to 2.5 m; 5 to 8 ft. high and wide) has a lovely solid, oval shape that does not require pruning. Its dense, glaucous blue mass is an excellent foil for deciduous shrubs with bright branches and for taller, drought-tolerant perennials like ornamental thistles, Russian sage, and echinacea that remain in the winterscape.

Montgomery spruce (*Picea pungens* 'Montgomery') is in the same size range as the globe blue spruce (4 by 1.5 m; 13 by 5 ft.), but more pyramidal when mature, as is *P. pungens* 'Bakerii' (3 by 1.5 m; 10 by 5 ft.).

The species (*Picea pungens* f. *glauca*) (30 by 15 m; 100 by 50 ft.) is best on large lots as a feature plant or used for windbreaks, massing, or hedging on acreages. Both *P. pungens* f. *glauca* 'Hoopsii' and 'Fat Albert' are slightly smaller, more narrow, and more silver-blue than the parent, growing to 12 m (40 ft.) tall. 'Fat Albert', at 6 m (20 ft.) wide, is more broadly pyramidal than the 2 m (6.5 ft.) wide 'Hoopsii'. Both 'Hoopsii' and 'Fat Albert' are grafted onto parent rootstock.

For unusual shapes, check out columnar *Picea pungens* f. *glauca* 'Fastigiata', weeping *P. pungens* f. *glauca* 'Pendula', or creeping *P. pungens* f. *glauca* 'Prostrata', which can mound, fall over walls, or be staked to create a weeping form.

Alternatives

If you want a globular shape and size, a mugo pine (*Pinus mugo*) works in the same cultural conditions. Consider various sizes of globe-shaped cedar (*Thuja occidentalis*) cultivars for sheltered spots. Dwarf cultivars of Norway spruce (*Picea abies*) that are similar in shape include 'Pumila' (1 by 1.8 m; 3 by 6 ft.), 'Nidiformis' (bird's nest spruce) (1 by 1.2 m; 3 by 4 ft.), which presents an inverted mound like a nest, and 'Ohlendorfii' (1.5 by 1 m; 5 by 3 ft.), which is slightly conical at maturity.

For the blue color, look at Rocky Mountain juniper cultivars such as *Juniperus scopulorum* 'Wichita Blue' or 'Medora' or savin juniper cultivars such as *J. sabina* 'Blue Danube'. *J. squamata* 'Blue Star', with its steel-blue needle clusters that resemble little stars, requires a sheltered, sunny spot to survive. *Pinus sylvestris* 'Glauca Nana' (2 by 2 m; 6.5 by 6.5 ft.) may work for gardeners with a sheltered location.

Pinus mugo var. mugo
(*Pee*-nus or *py*-nus *mew*-go var. *mew*-go)
Mugo pine

Plant at a Glance *(illustration pp. 36, 49, 128)*
   Type: shrub of the pine family (*Pinaceae*)
   Winter Features: evergreen, attracts wildlife, winter arrangements, architectural form
   Other Features: cones

Landscape Uses: mixed or shrub border, screening, feature or foundation plant, "bonsai" topiary

Height: 2 to 3.6 m (6.5 to 12 ft.)

Spread: 2 to 4 m (6.5 to 13 ft.)

Soil: poor to average, well drained

Light: full to part sun

Growing Tips: needs moist soil when young, but drought tolerant when established; let the needles lie where they fall as the shrub is self-mulching; control size by snapping new growth (candles) after growth spurt

Winter Density/Texture: dense/medium

Summer Density/Texture: dense/medium

Description

This native of central Europe is multi-stemmed, round to spreading in shape, and has medium to dark green needles in bundles of two. It is a dense plant in sun and more open in shade. Its height and width are extremely variable.

The plant can be purchased as "dwarf" (*Pinus mugo* var. *pumilio*), but it may be unaware of its title and quickly outgrow its suggested size. Assess future size at purchase time by both reading the label and examining the new growth (candle) length. Long candles are indicative of a faster-growing, larger shrub. Named cultivars are more likely to retain their dwarf size and are increasingly available. 'Teeny', 'Mops', and 'Slowmound' are all slow-growing cultivars that may grow to only 1.2 m (4 ft.) tall.

The taller mugos are excellent backdrops for the colorful bark and berries of deciduous trees and shrubs. Shorter forms are especially useful as understory shrubs for open-canopied trees and are attractive massed or as foundation plants.

Alternatives

Other mounding evergreens include globe forms of cedar (*Thuja* spp.) and Colorado globe blue spruce (*Picea pungens* f. *glauca* 'Globosa').

Several Norway spruce (*Picea abies*) also have dwarf, somewhat mounding cultivars. Bird's nest spruce (*P. abies* 'Nidiformis') (1 by 1.2 m; 3 by 4 ft.) has a slight indent in the center, 'Little Gem' (0.6 by 1 m; 2 by 3 ft.) is very dense, 'Pumila' (1 by 1.8 m; 3 by 6 ft.) is more spreading in form with upward-pointing branch tips, and 'Gregoryana' (to 1.2 m; 4 ft.) is broadly pyramidal. The Norway spruce prefers moist, well-drained, sandy soil and part shade, and is susceptible to drought and wind stress even when established.

Pinus sylvestris

(*pee*-nus or *py*-nus sil-*ves*-tris)

Scots pine

Plant at a Glance (*illustration pp. 29, 136*)

Type: tree of the pine family (*Pinaceae*)

Winter Features: shredding orange bark, evergreen, attracts wildlife, winter arrangements, architectural form

Other Features: curved cones

Landscape Uses: feature plant

Height: 15 to 20 m (50 to 65 ft.)

Spread: 8 to 12 m (26 to 40 ft.)

Soil: poor to average, well drained

Light: full sun

Growing Tips: drought tolerant when established; water deeply for the first two years; relatively disease and pest free

Winter Density/Texture: dense, but opening with age/medium

Summer Density/Texture: dense, but opening with age/medium

Description

The hardiness of Scots pines varies with their geographical origin; try to get plants originating from Scandinavia or northern Eurasia instead of western Europe. It has a "Christmas tree" form when young, but typical of pines, loses lower branches and inner needles as it ages. This "self-pruning" tree produces an open, irregularly shaped mature plant that many bonsai emulate in miniature. Its blue-green needles are twisted and held in clusters of two. They contrast well with its outstanding orange bark, which shreds and peels, becoming gray and furrowed with age.

The species is hardy and best suited to larger gardens. Its open nature and deep taproot permit under planting with other shrubs. There are several cultivars that are suitable for city lots. The sentinel-like columnar Scots pine (*Pinus sylvestris* 'Fastigiata') (to 7.5 by 2.5 m; 25 by 8 ft.) has a very upright branching habit. These branches can break under heavy, wet snowfalls, but this is not usually an issue on the prairies. 'Veridis Compacta' (1.2 by 1.5 m; 4 by 5 ft.) is a short, broad evergreen with green foliage, while 'Nana' (0.6 by 0.6 m; 2 by 2 ft.) is very small and suitable for rock gardens. Spreading 'Hillside Creeper' (0.3 by 2 m; 1 by 6.5 ft.) scrambles along and can soften the look of walls.

Scots pine
(Pinus sylvestris)
(p. 135)

Alternatives

Although no other pine offers the distinctive bark, try Swiss stone pine (*Pinus cembra*) (12 by 4.5 m; 40 by 15 ft.) or its dwarf form 'Nana' (3 by 1.5 m; 10 by 5 ft.) for similar hardiness, a more uniform shape, and dark green needles that are soft to the touch. This pine is very pyramidal when young, opening with age.

Bristlecone pine (*Pinus aristata*) (to 12 m; 40 ft.) is extremely slow growing and long lived. Specimens as old as 4,000 years are found in the southwestern United States. Its resin causes interesting white flecks on its needles. In spite of its height, it is bushlike because its moderately ascending main branches produce horizontal spokes of branches each year.

The very hardy yellow-green lodgepole pine (*Pinus contorta* var. *latifolia*) (to 12 by 3 m; 40 by 10 ft.) is a Rocky Mountain native more commonly grown on the western prairies.

Thuja occidentalis

(*thoo*-ja awk-si-den-*tah*-lis)

Eastern or northern white cedar (Arborvitae)

Plant at a Glance *(illustration p. 137)*

Type: shrubs and small trees of the cypress family (*Cupressaceae*)

Winter Features: evergreen, attracts wildlife, winter arrangements, architectural form

Other Features: strong structure, good background for perennials

Landscape Uses: mixed or shrub border, screening, feature or foundation plant

Height: 0.6 to 4 m (2 to 13 ft.), sometimes taller

Spread: 0.6 to 1.5 m (2 to 5 ft.)

Soil: average to fertile, moist, well drained

Light: part sun to shade

Growing Tips: situate in east and north exposures and provide extra screening if necessary; mulch heavily after planting; water heavily in early spring and again in fall starting mid-September until the ground freezes; water in winter if the ground thaws; new plants in slightly exposed sites may need screening until established; if shearing, avoid cutting back beyond new green stems

Winter Density/Texture: dense, but more open in shade/medium-fine

Summer Density/Texture: dense, but more open in shade/medium-fine

Description

Cedars, also known as arborvitae, come in a variety of sizes and forms, including columnar, pyramidal, and globe. Although most conifers tough enough to survive prairie winters have very hard needles, cedars have soft needles and a soft appearance in the garden. These trees and shrubs have flat branches with awl-shaped, scalelike leaves. Depending on the size of the cultivar selected, it can be included in a mixed border or used as a feature plant.

Hardy columnar and pyramidal cedar cultivars include 'Brandon' (to 6 by 1.5 m; 20 by 5 ft.), which forms a neat pyramid, 'Wareana' (Siberian cedar) (to 4 by 3 m; 13 by 10 ft.), which forms a broad triangle, and 'Techny' (to 4 by 2 m; 13 by 6.5 ft.), which has a very loose, open shape.

Hardy globe-shaped cedar cultivars include 'Woodwardii' (to 2 by 2.5 m; 6.5 by 8 ft.), 'Little Giant' (to 1.2 by 1 m; 4 by 3 ft.), and 'Danica' (to 0.8 by 0.8 m; 2.5 by 2.5 ft.).

Well-watered cedars maintain their freshness even in winter. Cedars make wonderful focal points in the winterscape due to their strong

Cedar or arborvitae, columnar and globe forms (Thuja occidentalis) (p. 136)
NORA BRYAN

architecture. They pair well with dogwood (*Cornus* spp.), highbush cranberry (*Viburnum trilobum*), and black chokeberry (*Aronia melanocarpa*), which require similar cultural conditions.

Many books recommend cedar for hedging, but countless gardeners have made the unpleasant and costly discovery that most places on the prairies are simply too windy and too dry. If you must try using it for hedging, you will have better luck on the eastern prairies where there is more summer precipitation and humidity.

Alternatives

To substitute for columnar and pyramidal cedars, consider Rocky Mountain juniper (*Juniperus scopulorum*) cultivars in sunny locations. Depending on the size of the globe you are considering, substitutes for globe cedars might include the various cultivars of mugo pine, juniper, and Colorado blue spruce. *Pinus sylvestris* 'Glauca Nana' (2 by 2 m; 5.5 by 5.5 ft.) may work for gardeners with a sheltered location. Finally, bird's nest spruce (*Picea abies* 'Nidiformis') can add a broad, flat-topped, horizontal form no taller than 0.9 m (3 ft.) as can shade-tolerant dwarf balsam fir (*Abies balsamea* 'Nana'). Both are less hardy than the preceding suggestions and require sheltered microclimates.

Twelve

Graceful Ghosts—Annual and Perennial Seed Heads

FLOWER SHAPES

Many plants, such as the poppy, have simple flowers, but others have clusters of flowers called inflorescences, arranged in various ways on the flower stalk. An inflorescence is described by its arrangement on the flower stalk, and some flower clusters have attributes of more than one arrangement.

Flower head: clusters of individual flowers appear to be a single flower directly attached to the flower stem, for example, sunflowers or purple coneflowers

Umbel: a flat or round-topped cluster in which all flower stalks arise from a common point, for example, allium; a compound umbel has smaller umbels branching from the main umbel, such as angelica

Spike: a flower stem with numerous flowers directly attached along its length, for example, liatris

Raceme: a cluster formed from a main flower stem with many unbranched side stems, for example, ligularia

Panicle: a cluster formed from a main flower stem with many branched side stems, for example, feather reed grass or astilbe

Allium spp.

(*ah*-lee-um)

Ornamental onion

Plant at a Glance (illustration p. 140)

Type: bulbous perennial of the lily family (*Liliaceae*)

Winter Features: spherical seed heads up to 10 cm (4 in.) in diameter, winter arrangements

Other Features: distinctive purple pompom flowers in late spring or early summer

Landscape Uses: perennial and mixed borders

Height: up to 1 m (3 ft.)

Spread: narrow

Soil: fertile, well drained

Light: full sun

Growing Tips: plant bulbs in fall; place lower-growing plants in front of the alliums to hide their fading foliage; some larger alliums decline on the prairies unless they are well fed and well spaced

Description

There are over 700 alliums, including onions and chives. Ornamental cultivars and hybrids are growing in popularity as gardeners discover their dramatic spherical flowers.

Spherical umbels of purplish pink to bluish flowers are held upright on tall stems in late spring to mid-summer, adding height to the garden display. In winter, the seed heads punctuate dried leaves and snowdrifts like upside-down exclamation marks. Stake dried seed heads in place to ensure that summer storms don't knock them down, or cut them down and save them for winter planters.

The best alliums for winter interest include the taller species.

Ornamental onion
(Allium aflatunense)
(p. 139)
NORA BRYAN

Allium aflatunense has purplish pink flowers, and its popular cultivar 'Purple Sensation' has violet flowers. Blue allium (*A. caeruleum*) (syn. *A. azureum*) grows 60 cm (24 in.) tall and has spherical umbels 2.5 cm (1 in.) in diameter. *A. cristophii* (syn. *A. christophii* and *A. albopilosum*), also called star of Persia, grows 30 to 60 cm (12 to 24 in.) tall with very large umbels—20 cm (8 in.) or more in diameter. *A.* x 'Globemaster' grows to 80 cm (32 in.), with deep violet umbels 15 to 20 cm (6 to 8 in.) in diameter.

It generally weakens over time on the prairies. Its amazing size makes it worthwhile to treat it as a biennial or short-lived perennial.

Alternatives

Globe thistle (*Echinops ritro*) has much denser, spherical seed heads.

Angelica gigas
(an-*gay*-lee-kah or an-*jell*-ee-kah gee-gas)

Angelica

Plant at a Glance

Type: short-lived perennial or biennial of the carrot family (*Apiaceae*)

Winter Features: dense, slightly rounded seed heads

Other Features: large umbels of deep red flowers in late summer or autumn

Landscape Uses: interesting architectural form, feature plant, pond side

Height: 90 to 120 cm (36 to 48 in.)

Spread: 60 cm (24 in.)

Soil: fertile, moist

Light: full sun to part shade

Growing Tips: it is a short-lived perennial or a biennial, so allow it to self-seed

Angelica gigas
LLYN STRELAU

Description

Angelicas are streamside woodland plants, native to the northern hemisphere. The related *Angelica archangelica* (food of angels) was regarded as an important plant with powers to cure practically all ailments.

Angelica gigas lives up to its specific epithet. It is one of the tallest plants that can be grown in a prairie garden. Large umbels of beet red blooms are held over large, coarse leaves that are deeply cut in three segments.

Alternatives

Joe Pye weed (*Eupatorium* spp.) also has great height and similarly shaped seed heads.

Artemisia ludoviciana

(ar-tay-*mis*-ee-ah loo-do-vee-kee-*ah*-nah)

Prairie sage

Plant at a Glance (*illustration p. 144*)

> **Type:** perennial of the aster family (*Asteraceae*)
> **Winter Features:** persistent silver foliage, seed heads
> **Other Features:** leaf texture, foliage color
> **Landscape Uses:** perennial or mixed border, rock garden, hot dry sites
> **Height:** 60 cm (24 in.)
> **Spread:** 60 cm (24 in.) or more
> **Soil:** poor to average, well drained
> **Light:** full sun
> **Growing Tips:** plant in in-ground pot with bottom removed to contain spread, if desired

Description

Artemisias are at home in the dry fields and prairies of the northern hemisphere. *Artemisia ludoviciana* is native to western North America, in the more southern parts of the prairies. Although commonly called sages for their aromatic leaves, they are not related to the culinary sages (the salvias)—don't cook with them!

Most artemisias are characterized by fuzzy, often lacy, silver foliage, which may persist well into winter. The late blooms are insignificant. Popular cultivars are 'Silver King', 'Silver Queen', and 'Valerie Finnis'. The latter is a less-aggressive spreader and may be more suitable in a mixed border with less-aggressive plants.

Alternatives

Artemesia stelleriana 'Silver Brocade' is a compact plant with almost prostrate stems, featuring very fuzzy, silvery white, scalloped leaves. The unrelated Russian sage (*Perovskia atriplicifolia*) has a similar color and habit in the winter garden. Cultivars of annual dusty millers (*Senecio cineraria* or *Centaurea cineraria*) "freeze dry" well for winter arrangements, seemingly impervious to the weather. The fuzzy stems and seed heads of lambs' ears (*Stachys byzantina*) have a similar silvery color.

Astilbe (hybrids of *A. japonica, A. simplicifolia,* and *A.* x *arendsii*)
(ah-*still*-bee ja-pon-ee-ka, sim-pli-ki-*fo*-lee-ah, ah-*rends*-ee-ee)
Astilbe

Plant at a Glance (illustration p. 144)
   Type: perennial of the saxifrage family (*Saxifragaceae*)
   Winter Features: rich brown plumes of dried seed heads, winter arrangements
   Other Features: airy blooms in mid-summer to fall
   Landscape Uses: shady places, pond side, mid to back of border
   Height: 30 to 90 cm (12 to 36 in.)
   Spread: 30 to 45 cm (12 to 18 in.)
   Soil: fertile, moist
   Light: part shade to shade
   Growing Tips: keep cool and moist; the more sun they receive, the wetter the soil must be; give these heavy feeders lots of compost supplemented by a balanced fertilizer several times in the growing season

Description

Wild astilbes inhabit mountainous ravines, woodlands, and stream banks of Southeast Asia and North America; the ones we grow in our gardens are complex hybrids and cultivars of several species. It seems unfair that the genus name comes from the Greek *a* meaning "not" and *stilbos* meaning "brilliant." Surely, the "not brilliant" flowers of the original species do not apply to today's elegant cultivars.

Astilbes are bushy plants with fernlike, divided leaves topped with airy panicles of creamy, pink, purple, or red flowers. Foliage ranges from light green to dark and glossy and the seed heads become deep russet. Collect them for containers where snow might flatten them.

Alternatives

Ural false spirea (*Sorbaria sorbifolia*) is a shrub that has conical panicles of white flowers held vertically over large, pinnate leaves. Consider some of the goatsbeards (*Aruncus* spp.) and their cultivars, as well as meadowsweet (*Filipendula rubra* 'Venusta') for similar plumy seed heads. Mature plants withstand winter's elements better.

Astilbe cultivars
(p. 143)
NORA BRYAN

This scene has it all: hard landscaping, changes in height within the border, and great contrast in color and texture. The blue spruce cultivar 'Hoopsii' is a foil for grasses of different heights and shapes, such as the panicum cultivar 'Heavy Metal' (p. 159), blue oat grass (Helictotrichon sempervirens) (p. 152), blue fescue (Festuca glauca) (p. 153), feather reed grass (Calamagrostis x acutiflora) (p. 144), a Blue Chip juniper, and the round russet mounds of potentilla and Goldmound spirea (p. 126).
BARBARA KAM

Artemisia sp.
(p. 142)
NORA BRYAN

Calamagrostis x *acutiflora* 'Karl Foerster'
(ka-la-ma-*gross*-tis x a-kew-tih-*flor*-ah)
Karl Foerster feather reed grass

Plant at a Glance (*illustration pp. 48, 160*)

Type: perennial of the grass family (*Poaceae*)

Winter Features: golden plumes, persistent foliage, architectural form, winter arrangements

Other Features: architectural form, movement

Landscape Uses: perennial and mixed borders, feature plant, perennial screen

Height: 120 to 180 cm (48 to 72 in.)

Spread: 60 cm (24 in.)

Soil: fertile, moist

Light: full sun

Growing Tips: tolerates a wide range of soil conditions; a great choice for windy locations where height is desired

Description

Reed grasses are a large group of northern hemisphere grasses, usually occupying marshes and damp woodlands. Our garden feather reed grasses are a hybrid of *Calamagrostis arundinacea* and *C. epigejos*.

Narrow panicles of bronzy or purplish brown inflorescence arise from a sturdy clump of tall, mid-green leaves. The leaves and inflorescence remain in place, dried to a golden color after the plant has died back to its roots. It stands sentinel-like even after heavy snowfalls, and the seed heads sway in the wind, giving both much needed height and movement to the winter border. Pair it with globe thistle or sea holly for a dramatic contrast in shape and tone that lasts well into winter.

Variegated feather reed grass (*Calamagrostis* x *acutiflora* 'Overdam') has white, pink, and green-striped leaves and forms a slightly smaller, looser clump than 'Karl Foerster'.

During spring cleanup, tie last year's tall seed heads and blades together with raffia and then cut them back to about 10 cm (4 in.). The grass bundle can be saved for use in next winter's arrangements. Not many perennial seed heads provide two seasons of winter interest.

Alternatives

Switch grass (*Panicum virgatum*) cultivars 'Heavy Metal', 'Strictum', 'Haense Herms', and 'Prairie

Globe centaurea
or giant knapweed
(Centaurea macrocephala)
(p. 146)
NORA BRYAN

Skies' have similar height and spread with open, airy plumes. They may not be hardy and may not develop inflorescences in the northernmost parts of the prairies.

Centaurea macrocephala
(sen-*tow*-re-ah or ken-*tow*-ree-ah mak-ro-*sef*-ah-lah or mak-ro-*kef*-ah-lah)

Globe centaurea, giant knapweed

Plant at a Glance (illustration p. 145)
 Type: perennial of the aster family (*Asteraceae*)
 Winter Features: knotlike seed heads, winter arrangements
 Other Features: thistlelike yellow flowers, cut flowers, attracts butterflies and bees
 Landscape Uses: back of the border
 Height: 90 to 120 cm (36 to 48 in.)
 Spread: 60 to 90 cm (24 to 36 in.)
 Soil: average, well drained
 Light: full sun
 Growing Tips: easily started from seed; its taproot makes it difficult to move, so plant it where you want it

Description

Globe centaurea is a native of the Caucasus and is named for centaurs, the half-man, half-horse creature of Greek mythology. Flagging centaurs munched the plant to restore vigor, sort of like a botanical Viagra™. This centaurea is a reliable, long-lived perennial with a deep taproot. The bold globe centaurea boasts bright yellow, thistlelike flowers held on stiff, tall stems covered with coarse, lance-shaped leaves. Unlike some other centaureas, it holds itself up nicely, so you can leave your twine and stakes in the shed. The dried seed heads remain standing in winter and resemble intricately crafted knots.

Alternatives

Scotch thistle (*Onopordum acanthium*) is somewhat taller, with thistlelike seed heads. Mary's or milk thistle (*Silybum marianum*) is a large, prickly plant with lovely white-splattered foliage, as though milk was spilled on its leaves, and attractive seed heads. It self-sows vigorously and is best harvested for use in containers. The statuesque annual cardoon (*Cynara cardunculus*) has very large, thistlelike seed heads.

Dipsacus sylvestris (syn. *D. fullonum*)
(*dip*-sa-kus si-ves-tris, D. ful-*lo*-num)
Teasel

Plant at a Glance *(illustration p. 148)*
Type: biennial of the teasel family (*Dipsacaceae*)
Winter Features: distinctive spiky seed heads, winter arrangements
Other Features: thistlelike, white or pale pinkish flowers, deer resistant
Landscape Uses: tall accent plant in a wild border
Height: to 150 cm (60 in.)
Spread: 30 to 80 cm (12 to 32 in.)
Soil: poor to average
Light: full to part sun
Growing Tips: easily grown from seed

Description
Teasel (*Dipsacus sylvestris*), a native of Europe and Asia, is not for fussy gardeners. It is rarely sold in garden centers because of its reputation for rampant self-seeding. Be prepared to cultivate in spring or remove seed heads for use in winter arrangements.

In its first year, teasel forms a rosette of toothy, dark green, lance-shaped leaves. The following year, tall stems with paired oblong leaves are topped with thistlelike, white or pinkish flowers. The flowers, arising in mid- to late summer may be up to 8 cm (3 in.) long. The oblong, pinkish purple flower heads are armed with dangerous-looking prickly bracts.

Alternatives
Globe thistle (*Echinops ritro*) and sea holly (*Eryngium planum*) have a similar prickly aspect to their flowers and seed heads.

Echinacea purpurea
(ek-in-*ay*-see-ah pur-*pew*-ree-ah)
Purple coneflower

Plant at a Glance *(illustration p. 148)*
Type: perennial of the aster family (*Asteraceae*)
Winter Features: prickly, thumb-shaped flower centers, attracts birds
Other Features: blooms late, attracts bees and butterflies
Landscape Uses: cottage garden, mid-border, perennial and mixed borders

Height: 90 cm (36 in.)
Spread: 45 cm (18 in.)
Soil: poor to average, well drained
Light: full sun
Growing Tips: young plants benefit from protective winter mulch; they are late appearing in spring, so it is best to leave your winter cleanup until they appear

Teasel (Dipsacus sylvestris)
(p. 147)
NORA BRYAN

Description

This native of the eastern United States is closely related to the prairie species *Echinacea angustifolia.* Some believe that the root of echinacea, taken orally, can ward off colds. Its name, from the Greek word *echinos* meaning "sea urchin" or "hedgehog," refers to the central spiny disk of the flower head.

This purple daisy has a pronounced central purple-brown cone (disc) and elegant downward-drooping purple petals (ray florets). Commonly available cultivars include 'Magnus', with flowers up to 18 cm (7 in.) in diameter and reddish purple petals that point straight out, rather than drooping downward, around a dark orange disc; 'Bravado', smaller, with rose-red petals; and 'White Swan', not surprisingly, a white form. The petals fall, leaving the central thumb-shaped, spiny disk, which retains a bronzy glow in the winter garden.

Purple coneflower
(Echinacea purpurea)
(p. 147)
NORA BRYAN

Alternatives

Cultivars of gloriosa daisies or black-eyed Susans (*Rudbeckia*) and prairie coneflowers (*Ratibida columnifera*) are similar, but their persistent seed heads are not as spiky as those of echinacea.

Echinops ritro

(*ek*-ee-nops *rih*-tro)
Globe thistle

Plant at a Glance *(illustration p. 149)*
Type: perennial of the aster family (*Asteraceae*)
Winter Features: distinctive large, spherical seed heads, winter arrangements
Other Features: globelike flowers, deer resistant, attracts butterflies

Landscape Uses: back of border, feature plant

Height: 90 to 120 cm (36 to 48 in.)

Spread: 60 cm (24 in.)

Soil: poor to average, well drained

Light: full sun

Growing Tips: prefers lean soil and lots of sun; if it is pampered with rich soil, it may need staking; it resents transplanting due to its deep taproot

Globe thistle
(Echinops ritro)
(p. 148)
NORA BRYAN

Description

Globe thistle is a native of south and southeastern Europe and central Asia. The genus name *Echinops* is from the Greek *echinos*, meaning "sea urchin" or "hedgehog."

Nothing else looks quite like globe thistle—its name describes it perfectly. If you have chanced upon a tall plant with coarse, prickly leaves and a perfectly spherical flower of steel-blue, purple, or white, then you know this plant. The seed heads are from 2.5 to 4.5 cm (1 to 1.75 in.) across. 'Vietch's Blue' is a commonly offered cultivar with a slightly smaller stature than the regular one. There is also a white-flowered globe thistle.

Globe thistle may not hold up well in nasty weather or under wet snows, but it dries well, so cut some in late summer and save it for winter arrangements.

Alternatives

Ornamental onions (*Allium* spp.) offer a similar "globes on sticks" look, while sea holly (*Eryngium planum*) provides similar textures and tones.

Sea holly
(Eryngium planum)
NORA BRYAN

Eryngium planum

(air-*in*-gee-um *play*-num)

Sea holly

Plant at a Glance

Type: perennial of the carrot family (*Apiaceae*)

Winter Features: distinctive prickly seed heads, winter arrangements

Other Features: attracts bees, metallic blue flowers

Landscape Uses: perennial or mixed border, specimen plant

Height: 76 to 90 cm (30 to 36 in.)
Spread: 30 cm (12 in.)
Soil: poor to average, well drained, dry
Light: full sun
Growing Tips: mulch plants well in winter where snow cover is erratic; due to its taproot, it resents being moved; may self-sow

Description

Sea holly is native to central and southeastern Europe and central Asia. This funky-looking plant does not appeal to everyone, with its prickly nature and alarmingly spiked flowers. Dark green, leathery leaves are topped with a forest of prickly, metallic branches and crowned by metallic blue, thistlelike flowers surrounded by a spiky ruff of blue bracts. The hybrid zabel sea holly (*Eryngium* x *zabellii*) has long dramatic bracts in blue violet. Plant sea holly in front of globe blue spruce with globe thistle for a charming winter vignette.

Alternatives

Teasel (*Dipsacus sylvestris*) and globe thistle (*Echinops ritro*) both have unusual prickly seed heads.

Gypsophila paniculata
(jip-*sof*-il-ah pa-nik-ewe-*lah*-tah)
Baby's breath

Plant at a Glance *(illustration p. 152)*
Type: perennial of the pink family (*Caryophyllaceae*)
Winter Features: architectural form, winter arrangements
Other Features: a light and elegant touch to a traditional perennial border
Landscape Uses: perennial and mixed borders, airy screening plant
Height: 60 to 90 cm (24 to 36 in.)
Spread: 60 to 90 cm (24 to 36 in.)
Soil: fertile, well drained
Light: full sun
Growing Tips: place this plant with thought, since like many plants with taproots, it resents being transplanted

Description

This baby's breath shares our garden with other related plants, including creeping baby's breath (*Gypsophila repens*) and the annual baby's breath

(*G. elegans*). Its genus name *Gypsophila* means "chalk lover," thus it likes our alkaline prairie soil. It is valued for its ability to screen out the dying foliage of plants that go dormant early, such as tulips, bleeding hearts, and oriental poppies.

In mid- to late summer, large panicles of tiny, white or pink, single or double flowers stand above loosely branching stems with fine, lance-shaped leaves. Commonly available cultivars include 'Alba', with single white flowers, 'Bristol Fairy', with double white flowers, and 'Pink Fairy', sporting double pink flowers. These plants need some support unless they are meant to ramble at leisure amongst other plants. They are excellent as dried flowers in winter arrangements.

Baby's breath is considered to be a nuisance weed in some places, and a noxious weed in Manitoba, because of its rampant self-seeding. Cultivating the soil around the plant or choosing double-flowered cultivars, which rarely set seed, can easily control it.

Alternatives

German statice (*Goniolimon tataricum*) and the similar-looking sea lavender (*Limonium latifolium*) both have flowers with an airy habit.

HE LOVES ME, HE LOVES ME NOT …

Daisies are well-known and well-loved flowers belonging to the huge family *Asteraceae*, formerly, the *Compositae*. Although a daisy appears to be a single flower of radiating petals surrounding a central disk, each apparent flower is actually several separate flowers (a composite) according to the rules of botany. Each petal that we pick when we desire to know true love is really the petal of a "ray" flower. Each ray flower has a collection of stamens and stigma, the male and female reproductive organs of a flower. The central disk is also composed of numerous individual flowers, called "disk" flowers, and each has its separate stamens and stigma. Easily recognized flowers such as sunflowers, coneflowers, and daisies belong to this family. Less-obvious plants like thistle also belong. Some composites only have "disk" flowers, such as *Rudbeckia* 'Green Wizard' and so we may not realize they are members of this family.

Helianthus annuus
(hay-lee-*an*-thus *an*-nyew-us)
Sunflower

Plant at a Glance *(illustration p. 152)*
Type: annual of the aster family (*Asteraceae*)
Winter Features: winter arrangements, attracts wildlife

A crabapple (p. 112) displays its branching form under a mantle of snow, while staked baby's breath (Gypsophila paniculata) (p. 150) holds its shape and adds a light touch to the foreground.
NORA BRYAN

Sunflower seed heads (Helianthus annuus) (p. 151) can be left in the garden or tucked into fences.
NORA BRYAN

Other Features: late-summer color, attracts butterflies

Landscape Uses: against a fence or foundation in a sunny cottage garden, containers, child's garden

Height: 30 to 180 cm (12 to 72 in.)

Spread: 60 cm (24 in.)

Soil: poor to average, well drained

Light: full sun

Growing Tips: sow seeds about 5 cm (2 in.) deep in spring after the danger of frost has passed and keep moist until seeds germinate; keep taller varieties out of strong winds and stake them

Description

Sunflowers are native to the Americas and have been extensively cultivated and hybridized for oil, seed, and ornamental plants. These very tall plants have unbranched or branched stems, with coarse, oval- to heart-shaped leaves. Large, daisylike flowers, up to 30 cm (12 in.) in diameter, come in shades of yellow, orange, and burgundy. Popular cultivars include 'Teddy Bear', with fuzzy-looking, double flowers, 'Russian Mammoth', with large, yellow traditional flowers, 'Big Smile', with large, golden flowers with black centers on short stems, and 'Autumn Beauty', with flowers in gold, brown, and red.

Although we don't usually think of the sunflowers as a winter plant, the seed heads are dramatic in winter arrangements or when woven into trellises.

Alternatives

The seed heads from other garden composites such as coneflowers (*Echinacea* spp.) and asters (*Aster* spp.) also provide winter seed for birds.

Helictotrichon sempervirens

(he-lik-to-*try*-kon sem-per-*vy*-renz)

Blue oat grass

Plant at a Glance (illustration pp. 44, 144)

Type: perennial of the grass family (*Poaceae*)

Winter Features: persistent fine, radiating foliage

Other Features: clump forming

Landscape Uses: accent or specimen plant, perennial or mixed border

Height: 90 cm (36 in.)

Spread: 60 cm (24 in.)

Soil: poor to average, well drained

Light: full sun

Growing Tips: water well until established, and then keep on the dry side; in spring, tug out the old seed heads and "comb" out the browned grass using a hand cultivator

Description

Oat grasses form a genus of about fifty species scattered about the temperate northern hemisphere on rocky slopes and gravel wastelands. Blue oat grass comes from western Europe. Its specific epithet, *semper-virens,* means evergreen. Stiff but finely textured, blue-gray leaves radiate from a neat clump year-round. Narrow panicles of oatlike, golden inflorescences arise on long stems well above the foliage in summer.

Alternatives

The smaller evergreen blue fescue (*Festuca glauca*) and its cultivars have similar color and habit.

Iris sibirica

(*eye*-ris sy-*beer*-ih-kah)

Siberian iris

The classic Siberian iris seed head (Iris sibirica)

NORA BRYAN

Plant at a Glance

Type: perennial of the iris family (*Iridaceae*)

Winter Features: rich brown seed pods

Other Features: graceful grasslike foliage, showy flowers

Landscape Uses: mid-border, moist places, pond side

Height: 60 to 90 cm (24 to 30 in.)

Spread: 15 to 76 cm (6 to 30 in.) or more

Soil: fertile, moist, well drained

Light: full to part sun

Growing Tips: top dress with compost annually; divide when the center of the clump dies out

Description

Siberian irises are natives of central and eastern Europe. Clumps of graceful, grassy foliage are topped by typical iris-shaped flowers (three upright petals, called standards, alternating with three downward-curving petals, called falls). Siberian iris comes in shades of purple or blue, and occasionally yellow and pink. Grasslike foliage may dry to a rich reddish brown or may die to the ground. However, the shiny, brown seed pods can be left standing or saved for winter arrangements.

Alternatives

Martagon lilies (*Lilium martagon*) have pale, candelabralike seed heads atop tall, slender stems.

Liatris spicata

(lee-*ah*-tris spi-*kah*-tah)

Blazing star, gayfeather

Plant at a Glance *(illustration p. 156)*

Type: perennial of the aster family (*Asteraceae*)
Winter Features: attracts birds, vertical seed head spikes, winter arrangements
Other Features: blooms late, attracts bees and butterflies
Landscape Uses: perennial or mixed border, vertical accent
Height: 50 cm (20 in.)
Spread: 45 cm (18 in.)
Soil: average, moist, well drained
Light: full to part sun
Growing Tips: quite drought tolerant once established; avoid winter wetness, which may cause it to rot

Description

Liatris is a North American native. *Liatris spicata* is commonly offered for sale at garden centers and is related to our more drought-tolerant native *L. punctata*, dotted blazing star or snakeroot.

Linear or lance-shaped, basal leaves surround a sturdy stem adorned with smaller, linear leaves. The shaggy, candle-shaped flower spikes come in lilac, purple, or white. Liatris has the peculiar habit of blooming successively from the top of the spike down, rather than upward as most flower spikes do. In winter, it maintains its flower color for some time if killing frosts come early.

Alternatives

Fleeceflower, bistort, or snakeweed (*Persicaria bistorta*) is a vigorous, moisture-loving perennial with pink, bottlebrushlike flowers up to 60 cm (24 in.) tall. The spikes are not as long as those of liatris. With soft, low-growing, silver foliage and pink flowers atop reaching stems, the seed heads of lambs' ears (*Stachys byzantina*) are also tall. The stems cannot withstand heavy snow, but they are attractive additions to winter arrangements.

Ligularia stenocephala 'The Rocket'
(lig-ewe-*lah*-ree-ah sten-o-*kef*-ah-lah or ste-no-*sef*-ah-lah)
Rocket ligularia, golden groundsel

Plant at a Glance (*illustration p. 156*)
   Type: perennial of the aster family (*Asteraceae*)
   Winter Features: spiky seed heads
   Other Features: very tall spikes of yellow flowers, bold foliage
   Landscape Uses: feature plant or back of a shady border, pond side
   Height: to 150 cm (60 in.)
   Spread: 100 cm (40 in.)
   Soil: fertile, moist
   Light: part shade to shade
   Growing Tips: the more sun they receive, the wetter the soil must be; an exposure with morning sun and afternoon shade is ideal

Description

This ligularia, sometimes called "elephant ears" owing to its very large leaves, is a native of northern China and Taiwan. It is a tall, imposing plant with large, heart-shaped, deeply incised leaves, topped by large spikes of late-blooming yellow flowers. In winter, the tall brown stems look best against a light background.

Alternatives

Ligularia przewalskii is very similar, although its leaves are smaller and more deeply lobed than 'The Rocket'. Mullein (*Verbascum* spp.) is a tall, spiky, somewhat brittle, and freely self-sowing alternative for a sunny, dry spot.

Ligularia
stenocephala
(p. 155)
NORA BRYAN

*Blazing star
(Liatris spicata)
(p. 154)*
NORA BRYAN

Miscanthus sinensis var. *purpurascens*
(mis-*kan*-thus sy-*nen*-sis var. pur-pew-*ras*-kenz)
Flame grass

Plant at a Glance *(illustration p. 157)*
Type: perennial of the grass family (*Poaceae*)
Winter Features: architectural form, cooked-rhubarb color with the pink tones lessening over the season
Other Features: orange-red fall color, movement
Landscape Uses: perennial, mixed, or shrub border, feature or foundation plant
Height: 60 to 90 cm (24 to 36 in.) without inflorescence
Spread: 45 to 90 cm (18 to 36 in.) without inflorescence
Soil: fertile, moist, well drained
Light: full to part sun
Growing Tips: cut to ground in spring; best color in full sun

Description
Originating in Japan and eastern Asia, this is one of the few miscanthus that performs on the northern prairies. It has 1- to 2-cm (0.5- to 0.75-in.) wide, green blades with purplish undertones, which first grow upright and then arch into a fountainlike form.

Although it does not usually flower on the northern prairies, it depends on the length of the growing season, moisture, and the warmth of autumn. Flowers are silver tassels that double the height of the plant and look like smoke rising from the flaming red-orange blades.

This grass retains its shape and color through heavy snowfalls and cold temperatures. It pairs well with the russets of spirea and

Siberian coral dogwood (Cornus alba 'Sibirica') (p. 104) and flame grass (Miscanthus sinensis var. purpurascens) (p. 156) display their vibrant winter colors.
JIM MICK

the blues and greens of conifers. The flaring shape echoes that of the weeping caragana.

Alternatives

Other grasses that prefer a moist culture include cultivars of purple moor grass (*Molinia caerulea*). For similar shape and color, look to the red switch grass (*Panicum virgatum*) cultivar 'Haense Herms' (to 1.2 m; 4 ft.). Two more hardy switch grass cultivars are the more erect and slightly spreading 'Heavy Metal' and 'Strictum', which is taller (to 1.6 m; 5.5 ft.) and becomes yellow in fall.

Monarda didyma

(moh-*nar*-dah *dih*-dih-mah)

Monarda, bee balm, bergamot

Bee balm (Monarda didyma)
NORA BRYAN

Plant at a Glance

Type: perennial of the mint family (*Lamiaceae*)

Winter Features: interesting seed heads

Other Features: those with red flowers attract hummingbirds, attracts butterflies

Landscape Uses: wildlife garden, back or middle of perennial or mixed border

Height: 90 cm (36 in.)

Spread: 60 cm (24 in.)

Soil: average to fertile, moist

Light: full to part sun

Growing Tips: select mildew-resistant cultivars and place them where they get lots of air circulation; give them good winter mulch; allow them to self-seed to ensure you always have these beauties around

Description

This monarda, a native of eastern North America, and its cultivars are the most commonly offered monardas at garden centers. The native prairie monarda, or horsemint (*Monarda fistulosa*), has lilac flowers and is more drought tolerant. Although the aroma of monarda leaves and flowers is strongly suggestive of Earl Grey tea, the tea's distinctive aroma comes from oil of bergamot, which is derived from the bergamot orange (*Citrus aurantium* subsp. *bergamia*).

Monarda has the characteristic habit of the mint family: square stems with alternate, opposite, lance-shaped, toothed leaves. The shaggy, mop-headed flowers come in shades of pink, purple, and red, depending on the cultivar. Some mildew-resistant cultivars include the hot pink 'Marshall's Delight' and 'Gardenview Scarlet', an older variety. The dwarf cultivar 'Petite Delight', with clear lavender flowers and growing only 30 cm (12 in.) tall, is suitable for the front of the border. Bees, butterflies, and humming-birds love the flowers. In winter, chocolate brown seed heads that last until January top the stems, unless early heavy snowfalls beat them down.

Alternatives

Phlomis tuberosa has similar flowers and seed heads, but stands much taller at 150 cm (60 in.).

Panicum virgatum

(*pah*-nee-kum vir-*gah*-tum)

Switch grass or tall panic grass

Plant at a Glance *(illustration p. 160)*

Type: perennial of the grass family (*Poaceae*)

Winter Features: persistent, upright foliage, attracts wildlife

Other Features: delicate airy inflorescence that sways in the wind, purple-brown flowers in late summer, attracts butterfly larvae depending on locale

Landscape Uses: accent plant, perennial screen, meadow or woodland edge garden, pond side

Height: 90 to 150 cm (36 to 60 in.) with inflorescence, depending on cultivar

Spread: 60 to 90 cm (24 to 36 in.)

Soil: fertile, well drained, moist

Light: full to part sun
Growing Tips: full sun for best coloration and form; tolerates wet to dry conditions in sand to clay soil; top dress with compost annually; cut back in spring;
divide every 3 years

Description

Panicum virgatum is a warm-season grass found on tall-grass prairies from
Saskatchewan to Nova Scotia and down to Florida, but it is most prevalent
on the Great Plains. Several well-behaved cultivars are suitable for the perennial border. The delicate burgundy flowers on stiff stems present an airy
froth above the blue-green grass blades. Fall coloration varies by cultivar. By
winter, blades are generally pale amber and the seed heads have lightened.

There are many cultivars. 'Haense Herms' is a smaller cultivar with
a fountainlike form and purple, vertical variegation on the leaves. The
leaves of 'Haense Herms' become red-purple in autumn, as do those of
'Rotstrahlbusch'. The glaucous covering on the lavender blue leaves of
'Heavy Metal' creates a metallic effect. It is slightly less hardy and may
suffer die-back, but recovers from its deep roots. 'Strictum' is one of the
tallest, most upright cultivars and also one of the earliest to bloom.

Switch grass partners well with other grasses, as well as yarrow,
monarda, and rudbeckia for late summer and winter interest in the border.

Alternatives

Cultivars of feather reed grass (*Calamagrostis* x *acutiflora*) provide similar height and movement to 'Strictum'. Flame grass (*Miscanthus sinensis*
'Purpurascens'), which does not always bear inflorescences on the prairies,
dries to a soft orange color like cooked rhubarb and is most similar to
'Haense Herms'. Tufted hair grass (*Deschampsia caespitosa*) and its cultivars
have airy, delicate seed heads but may not be hardy in zone 2. Cultivars
of purple moor grass (*Molinia caerulea*) come in a variety of heights, with
similar airy seed heads, preferring moist soil, as "moor" indicates.

Papaver spp.

(pa-*pah*-ver)
Poppy

Plant at a Glance (illustration p. 160)
    Type: annuals and perennials of the poppy family (*Papaveraceae*)
    Winter Features: thimble- or olive-shaped seed heads, winter arrangements

Other Features: large, single or double flowers

Landscape Uses: cottage garden, middle of perennial or mixed border

Height: 60 to 120 cm (24 to 48 in.)

Spread: 45 to 60 cm (18 to 24 in.)

Soil: average, well drained

Light: full sun

Growing Tips: most poppies self-seed quite readily; seed where you want them as seedlings do not transplant well

Cliffgreen
(Paxistima canbyi)
(p. 161)
NORA BRYAN

Description

The larger poppies, includ-ing the oriental poppy (*Papaver orientale*), the field or corn (Flanders) poppy (*P. rhoeas*), and the opium poppy (*P. somniferum*), have large seed heads that make great additions to winter arrangements. The oriental poppies offered for sale in garden centers are often hybrids with *P. bracteatum* (great scarlet poppy) and *P. pseudoorientale.*

Large, elegant, tissuelike flowers borne on narrow, hairy, nodding stems come in shades of white, yellow, pink, and scarlet. Basal leaves are grayish green and hairy and may be coarsely toothed. The thimble- or olive-shaped seed heads sport a crown of holes near the top, out of which the small black seeds can be sprinkled. Harvest seed heads while green and hang upside down in a cool, dry place.

Alternatives

Siberian iris has smooth, oblong, brown pods.

Poppy
(Papaver sp.)
(p. 159)
NORA BRYAN

Panicum virgatum
'Strictum' (left)
(p. 158) and Karl
Foerster feather
reed grass (right)
(p. 144)
JIM MICK

Paxistima canbyi (syn. *Pachystima canbyi*)

(paks-*ee*-stee-mah *kan*-bee-ee)

Cliffgreen

Plant at a Glance

Type: subshrub or perennial of the bittersweet family (*Celastraceae*)

Winter Features: retains leaves, leaves may turn bronzy in fall through winter

Other Features: small, dark, glossy leaves

Landscape Uses: compact shrub for woodland garden or a rocky wall, groundcover

Height: to 30 cm (12 in.), but usually shorter

Spread: to 45 cm (18 in.) or more

Soil: moderately fertile, humus rich, well drained

Light: full sun to part shade

Growing Tips: keep well watered in autumn; screen from drying winds; mulch lightly

Description

Cliffgreen is one of two genera found in mountainous places or coniferous woodlands of North America. Its alternative name is the unflattering "ratstripper." The other member of the genus, *Paxistima myrtifolia*, known as mountain lover or Oregon boxwood, is not hardy on the prairies. Cliffgreen sports small, fine-textured, glossy, oblong, toothy leaves. It is fully hardy on the prairies, but never grows very large. In winter, place this plant where it won't be completely covered by snow, but is protected from winter's worst drying winds.

*Russian sage
(Perovskia
atriplicifolia)
(p. 162)*
BARBARA KAM

Alternatives

Periwinkle (*Vinca minor*) also sports glossy, evergreen leaves. Gardeners on the southern prairies or those with an eye to "pushing the zone" might try creeping mahonia (*Mahonia repens*).

Perovskia atriplicifolia
(pe-*rof*-skee-ah ah-tri-pli-ki-*fo*-lee-ah)
Russian sage

Plant at a Glance (*illustration p. 161*)
Type: perennial of the mint family (*Lamiaceae*)
Winter Features: interesting architectural form
Other Features: late-blooming perennial forms a haze of lavender-blue flowers, attracts bees, pleasant fragrance when leaves are rubbed
Landscape Uses: a great filler plant in the border
Height: 60 to 150 cm (24 to 60 in.)
Spread: 60 cm (24 in.)
Soil: poor to average, well drained
Light: full sun
Growing Tips: great for hot, dry situations, but will thrive in garden scenarios where it gets enough sun; dislikes winter wet; wait until spring to cut back to live growth

Description

Although this native of Afghanistan is aromatic, it is not related to the artemisias, which we also call sages. It is related to the culinary sages (salvias), but it is not edible—so much for common names! *Perovskia* forms a bushy mass of grayish green, finely cut foliage. In mid- to late summer, branching spikes of tiny, lavender blue flowers appear. Its airy nature permits placement at the front of the border as a "see-through" plant, offering planned relief from lower-growing plants.

Alternatives

Sea holly (*Eryngium* spp.) has a similar habit and color, as does the denser *Artemisia ludoviciana*. English lavender (*Lavandula angustifolia*) has silver foliage and flower stems, but is shorter.

Rudbeckia spp.

(rood-*bek*-ee-ah)

Rudbeckia, orange coneflower, black-eyed Susan, gloriosa daisy

Plant at a Glance (illustration p. 48)

Type: short-lived perennials, biennials, and annuals of the aster family (*Asteraceae*)

Winter Features: dark, conical seed heads

Other Features: fall blooming, good cut or dried flower

Landscape Uses: perennial or mixed border, meadow gardens, attracts butterflies

Height: 25 to 80 cm (10 to 32 in.), depending on species and cultivar

Spread: 60 cm (24 in.)

Soil: moist, well drained

Light: full to part sun

Growing Tips: prefers full sun and moisture; adapts to dry soil; apply annual compost mulch; divide perennials in early spring; cease deadheading prior to killing frost for seed heads; leave basal foliage during spring cleanup; self-sows

Description

There are annual, biennial, and perennial coneflowers native to southern Canada and the United States. Black-eyed Susan (*Rudbeckia fulgida*) is one of the longest lived and most drought tolerant of the genus, although it prefers consistent moisture. Yellow-orange florets surround a brown-black, rounded cone atop multi-branching stems with shiny green leaves. The variety *R. fulgida* var. *sullivantii* 'Goldsturm' was the 1999 Perennial Plant of the Year. Its moniker translates as "gold storm," indicative of its abundant large flowers, which are 8 to 10 cm (3 to 4 in.) wide. It is more compact and sturdier than the species, with a dense habit that does not require staking. *R. fulgida* var. *speciosa* 'Viette's Little Suzie' is even shorter than 'Goldsturm'.

Single-flowering cultivars of the gloriosa daisy (*Rudbeckia hirta*) are great for winter interest. Cultivars include 'Indian Summer', 'Irish Eyes', 'Rustic Dwarf', 'Becky', and 'Gloriosa', which range in height from 25 to 90 cm (10 to 36 in.). *R. hirta* is generally an annual on the prairies, but may exhibit biennial habits.

The western coneflower (*Rudbeckia occidentalis*), a native of North America, grows to about the same height as *R. hirta*. Unconventional-looking cultivars include 'Green Wizard' and 'Black Beauty', which appear as if the petals have fallen off, even in bloom, and display a collar of green sepals around a long, narrow, brown-black cone. Their dramatic seed heads can be 5 cm (2 in.) in length, and are especially attractive in winter.

Rudbeckia's contrasting shape and color complement liatris, Russian sage, and ornamental grasses in both the summer and winter garden.

Alternatives

Prairie coneflower (*Ratibida columnifera*) (76 by 30 cm; 30 by 12 in.) has drooping, yellow petals surrounding a long, narrow, green cone that ages to brown. It prefers full sun and is drought tolerant. Biennial teasel has tall cones like the western coneflower, offering a spiky texture and lots of seeds.

Autumn Joy sedum
(Sedum x 'Autumn Joy')
NORA BRYAN

Sedum spectabile (syn. Hylotelephium spectabile)

(*see*-dum or hi-lo-te-*le*-fee-um spek-*tah*-bi-lee)

Showy stonecrop, showy sedum

Plant at a Glance

Type: perennials of the stonecrop family (*Crassulaceae*)

Winter Features: sturdy plant with good shape, attractive seed heads

Other Features: autumn color

Landscape Uses: hot, dry border, feature plant

Height: 30 to 45 cm (12 to 18 in.)

Spread: 45 to 60 cm (18 to 24 in.)

Soil: poor to average, well drained, dry

Light: full to part sun

Growing Tips: adapted to hot, dry situations; stems are easily broken off, but the broken stem roots readily

Description

Sedums form an enormous and varied genus, with members seemingly reclassified each time one dares to check. Doubtless, this name playing keeps many taxonomists duly employed, but we will ignore them all and continue to call them sedums.

This distinctive plant has thick, succulent stems and leathery, oval leaves of grayish green topped in late summer with flat heads of tiny, star-shaped flowers. The cultivar 'Autumn Joy' (syn. 'Herbstfreunde') has pink flowers that darken to copper. The similar 'Brilliant' has bright raspberry-colored flowers, while 'Matrona' has an overall burgundy tinge to both foliage and flowers. Cultivars with variegated foliage such as 'Frosty Morn' are becoming more available.

For shape in the winter garden, place tall sedums in front of evergreens in mixed borders or in front of taller, drought-tolerant plants that have attractive seed heads, like echinops or oriental poppies.

Alternatives
Both *Sedum* 'Vera Jameson' and S. 'Bertram Anderson' are lower-growing sedums. Their red-brown seed heads may poke attractively through snow cover.

Hen and chicks
(Sempervivum *cultivar*)
BARBARA KAM

Sempervivum spp.
(sem-per-*vee*-vum)
Hen and chicks, houseleek

Plant at a Glance
Type: evergreen perennials of the stonecrop family (*Crassulaceae*)
Winter Features: evergreen rosettes of thick, succulent, pointy but stubby leaves
Other Features: unusual flowers
Landscapes Uses: edging, rock garden, tufa container, crevices, groundcover
Height: 15 cm (6 in.) when in flower
Spread: individual plants up to 15 cm (6 in.), but mats form up to 50 cm (20 in.) in diameter
Soil: poor, very well drained
Light: full to part sun
Growing Tips: needs sun and superb drainage; will live happily in rock crevices and tufa dishes year-round

Description

Although succulent plants seem like they would be more at home in a hot desert, these little gems are extraordinarily hardy in prairie gardens. The species that produces most of our garden cultivars is the tough southern European native *Sempervivum tectorum*. It is also called the roof houseleek as it was sometimes grown on roofs, supposedly to ward off storms or lightning.

Small rosettes of leathery, stubby, pointed leaves form large mats. Leaf form and coloring varies, with leaf color ranging from emerald-green to bluish green to reddish, some with reddish margins or markings. The unusual clusters of star-shaped flowers form atop thick, "scaly" stems. A single rosette will soon propagate itself by sending out small rosettes on horizontal stolons. After flowering, the mother rosette dies, to be replaced by baby rosettes.

Alternatives

The native yucca (*Yucca glauca*) likes a similar situation and keeps its long rosette of blue-green, daggerlike leaves all year long.

Solidago 'Crown of Rays' (syn. 'Strahlenkrone')

(so-li-*dah*-go)

Crown of Rays goldenrod

Plant at a Glance *(illustration p. 168)*

Type: perennial of the aster family (*Asteraceae*)

Winter Features: sturdy light brown seed heads, attracts birds

Other Features: late blooms

Landscapes Uses: perennial or mixed border

Height: 60 cm (24 in.)

Spread: 45 cm (18 in.)

Soil: average, well drained

Light: full to part sun

Growing Tips: may need staking in rich soil

Description

Goldenrod cultivars, which are sometimes wrongly accused of causing hay fever, are the well-behaved hybrids of rowdy natives that spread pro-digiously by runners. As gardeners understand the true nature of these charmers, they are finding a place in many gardens.

The 'Crown of Rays' cultivar forms compact clumps topped by dense, bright yellow panicles of flowers. In winter, these sturdy, finely textured seed heads are enjoyed by birds. Some self-seeding may occur, but a bit of spring hoeing is a small price to pay for an extra season of interest.

Alternatives

Other named cultivars, such as 'Golden Baby' and 'Golden Wings', provide similar interest.

Vinca minor

(*ving*-kah *my*-nor)
Lesser periwinkle, creeping myrtle

Plant at a Glance *(illustration p. 169)*

Type: perennial of the dogbane family (*Apocynaceae*)
Winter Features: glossy, evergreen leaves
Other Features: star- or disc-shaped violet, purple-blue, or white flowers
Landscapes Uses: woodland groundcover
Height: 10 to 15 cm (4 to 6 in.)
Spread: many feet in all directions after several years
Soil: any relatively moist soil
Light: dappled shade
Growing Tips: locate under large, open-canopied trees; protect from drying winter winds by piling fall leaves loosely around and within the plant mass, still allowing the plant to be viewed

Description

Vinca minor is the only periwinkle that can be successfully grown on the prairies; the larger *V. major* is not hardy. Glossy, oblong leaves form on opposite sides of long, slender, trailing stems. In spring, and sometimes in fall, star-shaped flowers about 2.5 cm (1 in.) in diameter, in lavender, light blue, pink, or white, form on the leaf axils. *V. minor* will form a substantial spreading mat if sited in an area that it likes.

Alternatives

Cliffgreen (*Paxistima canbyi*) is another evergreen but much smaller plant that may be appreciated in areas of low snowfall. Creeping mahonia (*Mahonia repens*) offers glossy green, hollylike leaves for those gardening in zone 5 or for those who want to push the zone rating.

Yucca filamentosa

(*yook*-ah fee-llah-men-*to*-sah

Adam's needle yucca

Plant at a Glance *(illustration p. 169)*

Type: subshrub or perennial of the agave family (*Agavaceae*)

Winter Features: strong starburst form, evergreen

Other Features: spikes of waxy, cream flowers

Landscape Uses: feature plant, mixed or shrub border, rock garden

Height: 45 to 60 cm (18 to 24 in.)

Spread: to 90 cm (to 36 in.)

Soil: well drained, sandy

Light: full sun

Growing Tips: select a hot, dry site; hates standing water; may take years to bloom; may look tatty in spring; wear gloves when working nearby as leaves are sharp

*Golden clematis
(Clematis tangutica)
(p. 171)*
NORA BRYAN

*Lesser periwinkle
(Vinca minor) nestled
in a protective mulch
of fallen leaves and
mountain ash berries
(p. 167)*
NORA BRYAN

*Yucca glauca
rimed with hoar
frost retains its
unmistakable shape
(p. 168).*
NORA BRYAN

Description

Many yucca species have common names like "bayonet" and "dagger" due to their sword-shaped leaves. Adam's needle yucca is a nearly stemless plant with green, 4 cm (1.5 in.) wide, lance-shaped leaves that grow from a central rosette. As hinted at by its specific epithet, *filamentosa*, the leaves are edged in fine, curly threads. This plant will occasionally produce tall stems of downward-facing, waxy, bell-shaped flowers.

Alternatives

Native to southern Alberta and the northern plains of the United States, dwarf yucca, Spanish bayonet, or soapweed (*Yucca glauca*) (45 by 60 cm; 18 by 24 in.) resembles Adam's needle but lacks the filaments and has narrower, more glaucous leaves with whitish margins, producing a gray-green tone. Blue oat grass (*Helictotrichon sempervirens*) also has a radiating, spiky form, but with much finer leaves and texture.

Thirteen

Valiant Verticals—Vines

Clematis spp.
(*klem*-ah-tis or klem-*ah*-tis)

Clematis

Plant at a Glance *(illustration p. 169)*

Type: deciduous woody vine of the buttercup or crowfoot family (*Ranunculaceae*)

Winter Features: vine tracery, fluffy "feather duster" seed heads

Other Features: abundant colorful flowers

Landscape Uses: vertical interest for arbors, trellises, and fences, perennial or mixed border

Height: 2.5 to 10 m (8 to 33 ft.)

Soil: cool, fertile, moist, well drained

Light: full to part sun

Growing Tips: plant deeply in compost-enriched soil; keep roots cool by adding mulch or put shorter plants in front to provide shade

Description

Clematis has been called the "Queen of the Vines" for its spectacular flowers. It has been cultivated and hybridized for so long that the origins of some of our most popular hybrids are unknown.

The habit and form of clematis vary by species. In general, leaves are mid-green with three segments and are simple, lance shaped, oval, toothed, or fernlike. The flowers are usually shaped like an open saucer, star, or downward-facing bell, usually in shades of pink to purple to white. *Clematis tangutica*, the golden clematis, is very vigorous and has bright yellow, lantern-shaped flowers.

Snow highlights the complex weaving and twining of this vine's many branches. Additional winter interest is found in the fine, silvery, "feather

Virginia creeper
(Parthenocissus
quinquefolia)
(p. 174)
BARBARA KAM

Hops
(Humulus lupulus)
NORA BRYAN

duster" seed heads. Small birds also benefit from weather or predator protection amidst mature vines.

Some clematis, such as *Clematis alpina, C. macropetala*, and *C. tangutica* and their cultivars, do not need pruning except to control size, which can be done in early spring prior to renewed growth. Others, such as the large- and small-flowered hybrids, normally die down to the ground in winter on the prairies. Prune dead vines back to 30 cm (12 in.) in spring before new growth starts.

Alternatives

Fast-growing hops (*Humulus lupulus*) has interesting, but different, seed heads that look like little patio lanterns. It regenerates from its roots each season.

Humulus lupulus
(*hew*-mew-lus *loo*-pew-lus)
Common hops

Plant at a Glance
Type: perennial vine of the cannabis family (*Cannabidaceae*)
Winter Features: lanternlike seed heads, winter arrangements
Other Features: scratchy stems and leaves
Landscape Uses: privacy screen, fence or shed cover
Height: 6 m (20 ft.)
Spread: not applicable
Soil: average, well drained

Nightshade
vine *(Solanum
dulcamara) with
martagon lily
seed heads in
foreground
(p. 174)*
NORA BRYAN

Light: full to part sun

Growing Tips: likes moist springs and warm summers; cut back in spring; dig at least 30 cm (12 in.) down to cut the horizontal root to prevent spreading; susceptible to leafhoppers; easily propagated from softwood cuttings

Description

Law-abiding gardeners may be startled to find that common hops is the sole family relation to "black-sheep brother" cannabis. Hops earns its livelihood by giving the distinctive "hoppy" flavor to the legal substance beer.

An undemanding, extremely fast-growing vine, hops can grow as much as 30 cm (12 in.) on a warm day. Its herbaceous, very hairy stems and leaves can scratch and irritate the skin. It climbs by twining, always in a clockwise direction. Hops has very large, usually light green, three- to five-lobed leaves, although the cultivar 'Aurea' has yellow-green leaves. Female plants produce the attractive cone-shaped or lanternlike, green-gold flowers that are used to give beer its flavor. The vine can either be cut down and twined into wreaths or swags or be left intact for its attractive seed heads.

Alternatives

Other vigorous vines with big coverage are the golden clematis (*Clematis tangutica*) and the hybrid *C.* 'Prairie Traveller's Joy'. The woody Dropmore Scarlet honeysuckle (*Lonicera* x 'Dropmore Scarlet') is good for tracery, but does not have as interesting seed heads. It is drought tolerant and long blooming. Kiwi vine (*Actinidia kolomicta*) is another fabulous winter twiner for a sheltered area.

Parthenocissus quinquefolia
(par-tehn-o-*kis*-us kwin-kwe-*fo*-lee-ah)

Virginia creeper

Plant at a Glance (*illustration p. 172*)
  Type: deciduous woody vine of the grape family (*Vitaceae*)
  Winter Features: substantial twisted, twining stems on old specimens, small berries
  Other Features: red fall foliage
  Landscape Uses: wall or fence covering
  Height: 15 m (50 ft.)
  Spread: not applicable
  Soil: average to fertile
  Light: sun to light shade
  Growing Tips: very susceptible to the Virginia creeper leafhopper (Erythroneura ziczac), causing leaves to become patchy and eventually fall from the vine; usually not fatal, but ends any hope of beautiful fall color

Description

This garden favorite has large, five-lobed leaves and climbs using grasping tendrils. The cultivar 'Engelmannii' has sticky sucker pads that adhere to vertical surfaces. In winter, the strong woody vines present dramatic vertical sculpture against a fence or wall. Virginia creeper and the related Engelmann ivy are enigmatic plants that grow vigorously and large in some prairie gardens and barely struggle by in others.

Alternatives

Riverbank grape (*Vitis riparia*) or hardy grape cultivars such as 'Beta' and 'Valiant' have twining woody stems and blue fruit.

Solanum dulcamara (syn. *Lycianthes dulcamara*)
(so-*lah*-num dul-kah-*may*-rah)

Climbing nightshade

Plant at a Glance (*illustration p. 173*)
  Type: deciduous woody vine of the nightshade family (*Solanaceae*)
  Winter Features: vine tracery, red berries, winter arrangements
  Other Features: violet flowers all summer
  Landscape Uses: shady places
  Height: 3 m (10 ft.)

Spread: not applicable
Soil: fertile, moist, well drained
Light: full sun to shade
Growing Tips: easily started from cuttings or seed; drought tolerant once established

Description

"You let *that* grow in your garden!" may be the response of a horrified relative from Ontario or British Columbia, where this vine is considered a nuisance weed. In Washington state, it is a noxious weed. On the prairies, though, it can be contained, although some judicious hoeing may be required to prevent unwanted seedlings. Generally unavailable from garden centers, it is traded between gardeners with seedlings or cuttings to spare.

This useful shade-tolerant vine sports dark purple, star-shaped flowers with backward-facing petals similar to the flowers of the potato, its relative. Leaves are heart- or egg-shaped with two lobes at the base. There is a variegated form with cream-edged leaves. Because it is long blooming, the flowers and bright red, slightly oblong berries are present concurrently. The berries are somewhat poisonous—to what extent is debated by gardeners—so it is best not to eat them.

Climbing nightshade looks good sprawled on the ground or draped over walls. The bright persistent berries lend color to a wall or arbor.

Alternatives

American bittersweet vine (*Celastrus scandens*) has colorful seeds of red and yellow.

References

Books and CDs

Allen, Oliver E., and the editors of Time-Life Books. *Winter Gardens, The Time-Life Encyclopedia of Gardening*. Morristown, NJ: Time-Life Books, 1979.

Appelhoff, Mary. *Worms Eat My Garbage*. Kalamazoo, MI: Flower Press, 1982.

Barnard, Loretta, ed. *500 Popular Roses for American Gardeners*. Hauppauge, NY: Barron's Educational Services, 1999.

Bennett, Jennifer, and Turid Forsyth. *The Harrowsmith Annual Garden*. Willowdale, ON: Firefly Books Ltd., 1990.

Burton, Robert. *National Audubon Society North American Feeder Handbook*. Toronto: MacMillan Canada, 1992.

Glasener, Eric, guest ed. *The Winter Garden*, 47, no. 4 (Winter). Brooklyn, NY: Brooklyn Botanic Garden, 1991.

Harris, Paul and Terry Warke. *The Prairie Water Garden*. Red Deer, AB: Red Deer College Press, 1998.

Hillier, Malcolm. *Container Gardening Through the Year*. Toronto: Little, Brown, and Co. (Canada) Ltd., 1995.

Hole, Lois, with Jill Fallis. *Lois Hole's Favorite Trees & Shrubs*. Edmonton, AB: Lone Pine Publishing, 1997.

Hole, Lois, with Jill Fallis. *Perennial Favorites*. Edmonton, AB: Lone Pine Publishing, 1995.

Knowles, Hugh. *Woody Ornamentals for the Prairies*. Edmonton, AB: University of Alberta, Faculty of Extension, 1995.

Landscape Alberta Nursery Trades Association, Canada. *Trees for the Prairies*. Edmonton, AB: Author, n.d.

Leatherbarrow, Liesbeth, and Lesley Reynolds. *Best Bulbs for the Prairies*. Calgary, AB: Fifth House Publishers, 2001.

Leatherbarrow, Liesbeth, and Lesley Reynolds, with the Calgary Horticultural Society. *The Calgary Gardener, Volume Two: Beyond the Basics*. Calgary, AB: Fifth House Publishers, 1998.

Leatherbarrow, Liesbeth, and Lesley Reynolds. *101 Best Plants for the Prairies*. Calgary, AB: Fifth House Publishers, 1999.

Lenz, Louis M. *Woody Landscape Plants 47-003*. Winnipeg, MB: University of Manitoba, Continuing Education Division, Distance Education Program, 1996.

Lovejoy, Ann. *Ann Lovejoy's Organic Garden Design School: A Guide to Creating Your Own Beautiful, Easy-care Garden*. Emmaus, PA: Rodale, 2001.

Olds College Extension Services. *Prairie Horticulture Certificate: Landscape Design*. Olds, AB: Land Sciences Centre, Olds College, 1997.

Page, Susan, and Margaret Olds, managing eds. *Botanica: The Illustrated A–Z of Over 10,000 Garden Plants and How to Cultivate Them*. Vancouver, BC: Raincoast Books, 1998.

Pearman, Myrna. *Winter Bird Feeding*. Lacombe, AB: Ellis Bird Farm, 1989.

Pearman, Myrna, and Ted Pike. *Naturescape Alberta—Creating and Caring for Wildlife Habitat at Home.* Edmonton, AB: Federation of Alberta Naturalists, Red Deer River Naturalists, 2000.

Remphrey, Bill. *Woody Plants in the Prairie Landscape: An Interactive Guide.* St. Norbert, MB: Remphrey Botanical Publications, 1999. CDROM.

Schuler, Stanley. *Outdoor Lighting for Your Home.* Princeton, NJ: D. Van Nostrand Co., Inc., 1962.

Shaw, Tom, ed., *University of Alberta Home Gardening Course.* Edmonton, AB: University of Alberta, Faculty of Extension, 1986.

Taloumis, George. *Winterize Your Yard and Garden.* Philadelphia, PA: Lippencott, 1976.

Toop, Edgar, and Sara Williams. *Annuals for the Prairies.* Edmonton, AB: University of Alberta, Faculty of Extension, 1993.

Toop, Edgar, and Sara Williams. *Perennials for the Prairies.* Edmonton, AB: University of Alberta, Faculty of Extension, 1991.

Verey, Rosemary. *The Garden in Winter.* Boston, MA: Little, Brown, and Co., 1988.

Waldon, Bob. *Feeding Winter Birds.* Saskatoon, SK: Western Producer Prairie Books, 1990.

Williams, Robin. *The Royal Horticultural Society's Encyclopedia of Practical Gardening: Garden Planning.* London, England: Octopus Publishing Group Limited, 1999.

Williams, Sara. *Creating the Prairie Xeriscape.* Saskatoon, SK: University Extension Press, University of Saskatchewan, 1997.

Wilson, Helen Van Pelt. *Color for Your Winter Yard & Garden With Flowers, Berries, Birds and Trees.* New York, NY: Scribner, 1978.

Yakimovich-Parenteau, Virginia. *Prairie Landscape Design Guide.* Lloydminster, AB: Border City Graphics, 1990.

Articles

Doyle, Judith. "How Does Your Garden Grow?" *Calgary Gardening,* 10, no. 4 (May 1996): 17.

Kam, Barbara. "Container Gardens for the Winter Landscape." *Calgary Real Estate News* (December 1999).

Kam, Barbara. "Forcing Bulbs". *Calgary Gardening* (August/September 1998). [online]. Calgary Horticultural Society Article Archive Search. Available at: http://www.calhort.org/articles/index.cfm

Kam, Barbara. "Vermicomposting." *Calgary Gardening* (January 1997). [online]. Calgary Horticultural Society Article Archive Search. Available at: http://www.calhort.org/articles/index.cfm

Leatherbarrow, Liesbeth. "Want to Top It? Stop It!" *CHS Newsletter,* 8, no. 5 (June 1994): 6.

Power, Maureen. "Compost In The Winter? Sure You Can!" Calgary Gardening (October/November 2000). [online]. Calgary Horticultural Society Article Archive Search. Retrieved 5 September 2002 from http://www.calhort.org/articles/index.cfm

Power, Maureen. "Composting For Gardeners." *Calgary Gardening* (date). [online]. Calgary Horticultural Society Article Archive Search. Retrieved 5 September 2002 from http://www.calhort.org/articles/index.cfm

Leatherbarrow, Liesbeth. "Small Trees for Small Spaces." *The Gardener for the Prairies* (Fall 2001): 21–26.

Schroeder, Bill, and Nikolic Vesna. "Sea Buckthorn." *The Gardener for the Prairies* (Winter 1998): 30–31.

Svendsen, Erl. "Weepy, Droopy or Odd?" *The Gardener for the Prairies* (Winter 2000/2001): 36–39.

Williams, Sara. "Willows." *The Saskatchewan Gardener* (Winter 1997): 19, 20, 42.

Williams, Sara. "Ornamental Grasses." *The Prairie Gardener* (1999): 55–61.

Online

Alberta Agriculture, Food and Rural Development. Evaluating Woody Plants for Hardiness and Landscape Quality in Alberta (Last revised 11 January 2002). Retrieved 6 January 2003 from http://www.agric.gov.ab.ca/crops/trees/rwptp/

Althea_Z3_AB. "Plants for Winter Interest." Far North Gardening Forum. Retrieved 27 October 2002 from http://forums.gardenweb.com/forums/farnorth/

American Conifer Society. Introduction to Conifers. Retrieved 3 November 2002 from http://www.conifersociety.org/coniferinfo_frame.html

Burns, Marilyn. January 'Honey Do' List (1 January 2001). Retrieved 20 January 2001 from http://www.suite101.com/article.cfm/11370/87660

Calgary Horticultural Society Internet Chat Group

Chalker-Scott, Dr. Linda. The Myth of Antitranspirants. Center for Urban Horticulture, University of Washington. Retrieved 27 October 2002 from http://www.cfr.washington.edu/research.mulch/

Christensen, Jane A., and Donald Steinegger. Cedar-apple and Related Rusts of Apple and Ornamentals, G97-1327-A. Cooperative Extension, Institute of Agriculture and Natural Resources, University of Nebraska, Lincoln (May 1997). Retrieved 27 October 2002 from http://www.ianr.unl.edu/pubs/plantdisease/g1327.htm

City of Kanazawa. Yukitsuri—Rope supports for Protection from Snow. Retrieved 11 April 2002 from http://www.city.kanazawa.ishikawa.jp/custum_e/yukitsuri/yukitsuriE.html

Davis, Janet. Is Your Wreath Y2K-Ready? (28 November 1999). Retrieved 16 April 2002 from http://www.icangarden.com/document.cfm?task=viewdetail&itemid=1207&categoryid=27

Environment Canada. Canadian Climate Normals 1971–2000 (Created 17 December 2002. Modified 2 January 2003). Retrieved 7 January 2003 from http://www.msc-smc.ec.gc.ca/climate/climate_normals/index_e.cfm

Grupp, Susan. Forcing Branches Indoors. University of Illinois, Extension. Retrieved 7 October 2002 from http://www.urbanext.uiuc.edu/forcing/

Kabaluk, Todd. "Cedar Apple Rust." Gardenline Online. University of Saskatchewan, Department of Plant Sciences, Saskatoon. Retrieved 27 October 2002 from http://www.ag.usask.ca/cofa/departments/hort/hortinfo/fruit/rust.html

Koss, Walter James, James R. Owenby, Peter M. Steurer, and Devoyd S. Ezell. Freeze/Frost Data. Climatography of the U.S., 20, Supplement No. 1, National Climatic Data Center, Asheville, NC (January 1988). Retrieved 10 October 2002 from http://lwf.ncdc.noaa.gov/oa/documentlibrary/freezefrost/freezefrost.pdf

Monaghan, Barry, and Margaret Monaghan. The Winter Garden: Landscaping for Winter Interest. Retrieved 10 May 2002 from http://members.aol.com/monbj/ monbj/winter_garden.htm

Ohio Nursery & Landscape Association. Landscape Design. Retrieved 14 August 2002 from http://buckeyegardening.com/bglandscapedesign.html

Pellett, Harold, Nancy Rose, and Mervin Eisel. The Right Tree Handbook. Minnesota Landscape Arboretum, Department of Horticultural Science, University of Minnesota, Minneapolis. Retrieved 10 November 2002 from http://www.mpelectric.com/ treebook/

PFRA Shelterbelt Centre Publications. Repair of Snow and Ice Damage to Trees. Agriculture and Agri-Food Canada. (Reviewed 30 March 1999). Retrieved 5 October 2002 from http://www.agr.gc.ca/pfra/shbpub/shbpub45.htm

Purse, Lynn. Color in the Winter Garden (1997). Retrieved 10 May 2002 from www.creativegardener.com/winter.html

"Rochester's History—An Illustrated Timeline." Glossary of Victorian Cemetery Symbolism. Retrieved 17 April 2002 from http://www.vintageviews.org/vv-tl/pages/ Cem_Symbolism.htm#plants

Shaffer, W. Hal, and James Allen Wrather. "Cedar Apple Rust." Agricultural Publication G7870—Revised February 15, 1996. Department of Plant Pathology, University of Missouri-Columbia. Retrieved 27 October 2002 from http:// muextension.missouri.edu/xplor/agguides/pests/g07870.htm

Silzer, Tanya. "Panicum virgatum L." Rangeland Ecosystems & Plants: Fact Sheets For Some Common Plants On Rangelands In Western Canada. Retrieved 31 January 2003 from http://www.usask.ca/agriculture/plantsci/classes/range/panicum.html

St-Pierre, Richard. "The Highbush Cranberry—A Multipurpose Shrub." Gardenline Online. University of Saskatchewan, Department of Plant Sciences, Saskatoon (1995). Retrieved 10 November 2001 from http://www.ag.usask.ca/cofa/departments/hort/ hortinfo/fruit/cranbery.html

Talt, Marge. Form in the Garden (22 December 1998). Retrieved 13 November 2001 from http://www.suite101.com/article.cfm/222/13865

3482—Forcing Branches of Spring-flowering Plants. Kemper Center for Home Gardening. Retrieved 7 October 2002 from http://www.mobot.org/gardeninghelp/ hortline/messages/3482.shtml

Wood, Grant. "Prune Your Cedars Cautiously." Gardenline Online. University of Saskatchewan, Department of Plant Sciences, Saskatoon. Retrieved 30 November 2002 from http://www.ag.usask.ca/cofa/departments/hort/hortinfo/trees/cedars.html

Index

In this index, numbers appearing in Roman bold type (e.g., **125**) indicates a main entry; italic bold type (e.g., *44*) indicate an illustration, and square brackets (e.g., [187]) indicate a table entry.